Natural Language Processing with Java

Explore various approaches to organize and extract useful text from unstructured data using Java

Richard M Reese

BIRMINGHAM - MUMBAI

Natural Language Processing with Java

First published: March 2015

Production reference: 1170315

Published by Packt Publishing Ltd.
Livery Place
35 Livery Street
Birmingham B3 2PB, UK.

ISBN 978-1-78439-179-9

www.packtpub.com

Credits

Author

Richard M Reese

Reviewers

Suryaprakash CV

Evan Dempsey

Anil Omanwar

Amitabh Sharma

Commissioning Editor

Nadeem N. Bagban

Acquisition Editor

Sonali Vernekar

Content Development Editor

Ritika Singh

Technical Editor

Manali Gonsalves

Copy Editors

Pranjali Chury

Vikrant Phadke

Project Coordinators

Aboli Ambardekar

Judie Jose

Proofreaders

Simran Bhogal

Jonathan Todd

Indexer

Priya Sane

Production Coordinator

Nitesh Thakur

Cover Work

Nitesh Thakur

About the Author

Richard M Reese has worked in both industry and academics. For 17 years, he worked in the telephone and aerospace industries, serving in several capacities, including research and development, software development, supervision, and training. He currently teaches at Tarleton State University, where he is able to apply his years of industry experience to enhance his classes.

Richard has written several Java and C books. He uses a concise and easy-to-follow approach to topics at hand. His books include *EJB 3.1 Cookbook*; books about new features of Java 7 and 8, Java Certification, and jMonkey Engine; and a book on C pointers.

I would like to thank my daughter, Jennifer, for the numerous reviews and contributions she has made. Her input has been invaluable.

About the Reviewers

Suryaprakash C.V. has been working in the field of NLP since 2009. He has done his graduation in physics and postgraduation in computer applications. Later, he got an opportunity to pursue a career in his area of interest, which is natural language processing.

Currently, Suryaprakash is a research lead at Senseforth Technologies.

> I would like to thank my colleagues for supporting me in my career and job. It helped me a lot in this review process.

Evan Dempsey is a software developer from Waterford, Ireland. When he isn't hacking using Python for fun and profit, he enjoys craft beers, Common Lisp, and keeping up with modern research in machine learning. He is a contributor to several open source projects.

Anil Omanwar is a dynamic personality with a great passion for the hottest technology trends and research. He has more than 8 years of experience in researching cognitive computing. Natural language processing, machine learning, information visualization, and text analytics are a few key areas of his research interests.

He is proficient in sentiment analysis, questionnaire-based feedback, text clustering, and phrase extraction in diverse domains, such as life sciences, manufacturing, retail, e-commerce, hospitality, customer relations, banking, and social media.

Anil is currently associated with IBM labs for NLP and IBM Watson in the life sciences domain. The objective of his research is to automate critical manual steps and assist domain experts in optimizing human-machine capabilities.

In his spare time, he enjoys working for social causes, trekking, photography, and traveling. He is always ready to take up technical challenges.

Amitabh Sharma is a professional software engineer. He has worked extensively on enterprise applications in telecommunications and business analytics. His work has focused on service-oriented architecture, data warehouses, and languages such as Java, Python, and so on.

www.PacktPub.com

Support files, eBooks, discount offers, and more

For support files and downloads related to your book, please visit www.PacktPub.com.

Did you know that Packt offers eBook versions of every book published, with PDF and ePub files available? You can upgrade to the eBook version at www.PacktPub.com and as a print book customer, you are entitled to a discount on the eBook copy. Get in touch with us at service@packtpub.com for more details.

At www.PacktPub.com, you can also read a collection of free technical articles, sign up for a range of free newsletters and receive exclusive discounts and offers on Packt books and eBooks.

https://www2.packtpub.com/books/subscription/packtlib

Do you need instant solutions to your IT questions? PacktLib is Packt's online digital book library. Here, you can search, access, and read Packt's entire library of books.

Why subscribe?

- Fully searchable across every book published by Packt
- Copy and paste, print, and bookmark content
- On demand and accessible via a web browser

Free access for Packt account holders

If you have an account with Packt at www.PacktPub.com, you can use this to access PacktLib today and view 9 entirely free books. Simply use your login credentials for immediate access.

Table of Contents

Preface

Natural Language Processing (NLP) has been used to address a wide range of problems, including support for search engines, summarizing and classifying text for web pages, and incorporating machine learning technologies to solve problems such as speech recognition and query analysis. It has found use wherever documents contain useful information.

NLP is used to enhance the utility and power of applications. It does so by making user input easier and converting text to more usable forms. In essence, NLP processes natural text found in a variety of sources, using a series of core NLP tasks to transform or extract information from the text.

This book focuses on core NLP tasks that will likely be encountered in an NLP application. Each NLP task presented in this book starts with a description of the problem and where it can be used. The issues that make each task difficult are introduced so that you can understand the problem in a better way. This is followed by the use of numerous Java techniques and APIs to support an NLP task.

What this book covers

Chapter 1, Introduction to NLP, explains the importance and uses of NLP. The NLP techniques used in this chapter are explained with simple examples illustrating their use.

Chapter 2, Finding Parts of Text, focuses primarily on tokenization. This is the first step in more advanced NLP tasks. Both core Java and Java NLP tokenization APIs are illustrated.

Chapter 3, Finding Sentences, proves that sentence boundary disambiguation is an important NLP task. This step is a precursor for many other downstream NLP tasks where text elements should not be split across sentence boundaries. This includes ensuring that all phrases are in one sentence and supporting parts of speech analysis.

Chapter 4, Finding People and Things, covers what is commonly referred to as Named Entity Recognition. This task is concerned with identifying people, places, and similar entities in text. This technique is a preliminary step for processing queries and searches.

Chapter 5, Detecting Parts of Speech, shows you how to detect parts of speech, which are grammatical elements of text, such as nouns and verbs. Identifying these elements is a significant step in determining the meaning of text and detecting relationships within text.

Chapter 6, Classifying Texts and Documents, proves that classifying text is useful for tasks such as spam detection and sentiment analysis. The NLP techniques that support this process are investigated and illustrated.

Chapter 7, Using Parser to Extract Relationships, demonstrates parse trees. A parse tree is used for many purposes, including information extraction. It holds information regarding the relationships between these elements. An example implementing a simple query is presented to illustrate this process.

Chapter 8, Combined Approaches, contains techniques for extracting data from various types of documents, such as PDF and Word files. This is followed by an examination of how the previous NLP techniques can be combined into a pipeline to solve larger problems.

What you need for this book

Java SDK 7 is used to illustrate the NLP techniques. Various NLP APIs are needed and can be readily downloaded. An IDE is not required but is desirable.

Who this book is for

Experienced Java developers who are interested in NLP techniques will find this book useful. No prior exposure to NLP is required.

Conventions

In this book, you will find a number of styles of text that distinguish between different kinds of information. Here are some examples of these styles, and explanations of their meanings.

Code words in text are shown as follows: "The keyset method returns a set of all the annotation keys currently held by the Annotation object."

Database table names, folder names, filenames, file extensions, pathnames, dummy URLs, user input, and Twitter handles are shown as follows: "To demonstrate the use of POI, we will use a file called TestDocument.pdf."

A block of code is set as follows:

```
for (int index = 0; index < sentences.length; index++) {
    String tokens[] = tokenizer.tokenize(sentences[index]);
    Span nameSpans[] = nameFinder.find(tokens);
    for(Span span : nameSpans) {
        list.add("Sentence: " + index
            + " Span: " + span.toString() + " Entity: "
            + tokens[span.getStart()]);
    }
}
```

The output of code sequences looks like what is shown here:

```
Sentence: 0 Span: [0..1) person Entity: Joe
Sentence: 0 Span: [7..9) person Entity: Fred
Sentence: 2 Span: [0..1) person Entity: Joe
```

New terms and **important words** are shown in bold.

 Warnings or important notes appear in a box like this.

 Tips and tricks appear like this.

Reader feedback

Feedback from our readers is always welcome. Let us know what you think about this book—what you liked or disliked. Reader feedback is important for us as it helps us develop titles that you will really get the most out of.

To send us general feedback, simply e-mail feedback@packtpub.com, and mention the book's title in the subject of your message.

If there is a topic that you have expertise in and you are interested in either writing or contributing to a book, see our author guide at www.packtpub.com/authors.

Customer support

Now that you are the proud owner of a Packt book, we have a number of things to help you to get the most from your purchase.

Downloading the example code

You can download the example code files for all Packt books you have purchased from your account at http://www.packtpub.com. If you purchased this book elsewhere, you can visit http://www.packtpub.com/support and register to have the files e-mailed directly to you.

Errata

Although we have taken every care to ensure the accuracy of our content, mistakes do happen. If you find a mistake in one of our books—maybe a mistake in the text or the code—we would be grateful if you would report this to us. By doing so, you can save other readers from frustration and help us improve subsequent versions of this book. If you find any errata, please report them by visiting http://www.packtpub.com/submit-errata, selecting your book, clicking on the **errata submission form** link, and entering the details of your errata. Once your errata are verified, your submission will be accepted and the errata will be uploaded on our website, or added to any list of existing errata, under the Errata section of that title. Any existing errata can be viewed by selecting your title from http://www.packtpub.com/support.

Piracy

Piracy of copyrighted material on the Internet is an ongoing problem across all media. At Packt, we take the protection of our copyright and licenses very seriously. If you come across any illegal copies of our works in any form on the Internet, please provide us with the location address or website name immediately so that we can pursue a remedy.

Please contact us at copyright@packtpub.com with a link to the suspected pirated material.

We appreciate your help in protecting our authors and our ability to bring you valuable content.

Questions

If you have a problem with any aspect of this book, you can contact us at questions@packtpub.com, and we will do our best to address the problem.

1
Introduction to NLP

Natural Language Processing (NLP) is a broad topic focused on the use of computers to analyze natural languages. It addresses areas such as speech processing, relationship extraction, document categorization, and summation of text. However, these types of analysis are based on a set of fundamental techniques such as tokenization, sentence detection, classification, and extracting relationships. These basic techniques are the focus of this book. We will start with a detailed discussion of NLP, investigate why it is important, and identify application areas.

There are many tools available that support NLP tasks. We will focus on the Java language and how various Java **Application Programmer Interfaces (APIs)** support NLP. In this chapter, we will briefly identify the major APIs, including Apache's OpenNLP, Stanford NLP libraries, LingPipe, and GATE.

This is followed by a discussion of the basic NLP techniques illustrated in this book. The nature and use of these techniques is presented and illustrated using one of the NLP APIs. Many of these techniques will use models. Models are similar to a set of rules that are used to perform a task such as tokenizing text. They are typically represented by a class that is instantiated from a file. We round off the chapter with a brief discussion on how data can be prepared to support NLP tasks.

NLP is not easy. While some problems can be solved relatively easily, there are many others that require the use of sophisticated techniques. We will strive to provide a foundation for NLP processing so that you will be able to understand better which techniques are available and applicable for a given problem.

NLP is a large and complex field. In this book, we will only be able to address a small part of it. We will focus on core NLP tasks that can be implemented using Java. Throughout this book, we will demonstrate a number of NLP techniques using both the Java SE SDK and other libraries, such as OpenNLP and Stanford NLP. To use these libraries, there are specific API JAR files that need to be associated with the project in which they are being used. A discussion of these libraries is found in the Survey of NLP tools section and contains download links to the libraries. The examples in this book were developed using NetBeans 8.0.2. These projects required the API JAR files to be added to the Libraries category of the Projects Properties dialog box.

What is NLP?

A formal definition of NLP frequently includes wording to the effect that it is a field of study using computer science, artificial intelligence, and formal linguistics concepts to analyze natural language. A less formal definition suggests that it is a set of tools used to derive meaningful and useful information from natural language sources such as web pages and text documents.

Meaningful and useful implies that it has some commercial value, though it is frequently used for academic problems. This can readily be seen in its support of search engines. A user query is processed using NLP techniques in order to generate a result page that a user can use. Modern search engines have been very successful in this regard. NLP techniques have also found use in automated help systems and in support of complex query systems as typified by IBM's Watson project.

When we work with a language, the terms, syntax, and semantics, are frequently encountered. The syntax of a language refers to the rules that control a valid sentence structure. For example, a common sentence structure in English starts with a subject followed by a verb and then an object such as "Tim hit the ball". We are not used to unusual sentence order such as "Hit ball Tim". Although the rule of syntax for English is not as rigorous as that for computer languages, we still expect a sentence to follow basic syntax rules.

The semantics of a sentence is its meaning. As English speakers, we understand the meaning of the sentence "Tim hit the ball". However, English and other natural languages can be ambiguous at times and a sentence's meaning may only be determined from its context. As we will see, various machine learning techniques can be used to attempt to derive the meaning of text.

As we progress with our discussions, we will introduce many linguistic terms that will help us better understand natural languages and provide us with a common vocabulary to explain the various NLP techniques. We will see how the text can be split into individual elements and how these elements can be classified.

In general, these approaches are used to enhance applications, thus making them more valuable to their users. The uses of NLP can range from relatively simple uses to those that are pushing what is possible today. In this book, we will show examples that illustrate simple approaches, which may be all that is required for some problems, to the more advanced libraries and classes available to address sophisticated needs.

Why use NLP?

NLP is used in a wide variety of disciplines to solve many different types of problems. Text analysis is performed on text that ranges from a few words of user input for an Internet query to multiple documents that need to be summarized. We have seen a large growth in the amount and availability of unstructured data in recent years. This has taken forms such as blogs, tweets, and various other social media. NLP is ideal for analyzing this type of information.

Machine learning and text analysis are used frequently to enhance an application's utility. A brief list of application areas follow:

- **Searching**: This identifies specific elements of text. It can be as simple as finding the occurrence of a name in a document or might involve the use of synonyms and alternate spelling/misspelling to find entries that are close to the original search string.

- **Machine translation**: This typically involves the translation of one natural language into another.

- **Summation**: Paragraphs, articles, documents, or collections of documents may need to be summarized. NLP has been used successfully for this purpose.

- **Named Entity Recognition (NER)**: This involves extracting names of locations, people, and things from text. Typically, this is used in conjunction with other NLP tasks such as processing queries.

- **Information grouping**: This is an important activity that takes textual data and creates a set of categories that reflect the content of the document. You have probably encountered numerous websites that organize data based on your needs and have categories listed on the left-hand side of the website.

- **Parts of Speech Tagging (POS)**: In this task, text is split up into different grammatical elements such as nouns and verbs. This is useful in analyzing the text further.

- **Sentiment analysis**: People's feelings and attitudes regarding movies, books, and other products can be determined using this technique. This is useful in providing automated feedback with regards to how well a product is perceived.

- **Answering queries**: This type of processing was illustrated when IBM's Watson successfully won a Jeopardy competition. However, its use is not restricted to winning game shows and has been used in a number of other fields including medicine.

- **Speech recognition**: Human speech is difficult to analyze. Many of the advances that have been made in this field are the result of NLP efforts.

- **Natural Language Generation**: This is the process of generating text from a data or knowledge source, such as a database. It can automate reporting of information such as weather reports, or summarize medical reports.

NLP tasks frequently use different machine learning techniques. A common approach starts with training a model to perform a task, verifying that the model is correct, and then applying the model to a problem. We will examine this process further in *Understanding NLP models* later in the chapter.

Why is NLP so hard?

NLP is not easy. There are several factors that makes this process hard. For example, there are hundreds of natural languages, each of which has different syntax rules. Words can be ambiguous where their meaning is dependent on their context. Here, we will examine a few of the more significant problem areas.

At the character level, there are several factors that need to be considered. For example, the encoding scheme used for a document needs to be considered. Text can be encoded using schemes such as ASCII, UTF-8, UTF-16, or Latin-1. Other factors such as whether the text should be treated as case-sensitive or not may need to be considered. Punctuation and numbers may require special processing. We sometimes need to consider the use of emoticons (character combinations and special character images), hyperlinks, repeated punctuation (… or ---), file extension, and usernames with embedded periods. Many of these are handled by preprocessing text as we will discuss in *Preparing data* later in the chapter.

When we **Tokenize** text, it usually means we are breaking up the text into a sequence of words. These words are called **Tokens**. The process is referred to as **Tokenization**. When a language uses whitespace characters to delineate words, this process is not too difficult. With a language like Chinese, it can be quite difficult since it uses unique symbols for words.

Words and morphemes may need to be assigned a part of speech label identifying what type of unit it is. A **Morpheme** is the smallest division of text that has meaning. Prefixes and suffixes are examples of morphemes. Often, we need to consider synonyms, abbreviation, acronyms, and spellings when we work with words.

Stemming is another task that may need to be applied. **Stemming** is the process of finding the word stem of a word. For example, words such as "walking", "walked", or "walks" have the word stem "walk". Search engines often use stemming to assist in asking a query.

Closely related to stemming is the process of **Lemmatization**. This process determines the base form of a word called its **lemma**. For example, for the word "operating", its stem is "oper" but its lemma is "operate". Lemmatization is a more refined process than stemming and uses vocabulary and morphological techniques to find a lemma. This can result in more precise analysis in some situations.

Words are combined into phrases and sentences. Sentence detection can be problematic and is not as simple as looking for the periods at the end of a sentence. Periods are found in many places including abbreviations such as Ms. and in numbers such as 12.834.

We often need to understand which words in a sentence are nouns and which are verbs. We are sometimes concerned with the relationship between words. For example, **Coreferences resolution** determines the relationship between certain words in one or more sentences. Consider the following sentence:

"The city is large but beautiful. It fills the entire valley."

The word "it" is the coreference to city. When a word has multiple meanings we might need to perform **Word Sense Disambiguation** to determine the meaning that was intended. This can be difficult to do at times. For example, "John went back home".

Does the home refer to a house, a city, or some other unit? Its meaning can sometimes be inferred from the context in which it is used. For example, "John went back home. It was situated at the end of a cul-de-sac."

In spite of these difficulties, NLP is able to perform these tasks reasonably well in most situations and provide added value to many problem domains. For example, sentiment analysis can be performed on customer tweets resulting in possible free product offers for dissatisfied customers. Medical documents can be readily summarized to highlight the relevant topics and improved productivity.

Summarization is the process of producing a short description of different units. These units can include multiple sentences, paragraphs, a document, or multiple documents. The intent may be to identify those sentences that convey the meaning of the unit, determine the prerequisites for understanding a unit, or to find items within these units. Frequently, the context of the text is important in accomplishing this task.

Survey of NLP tools

There are many tools available that support NLP. Some of these are available with the Java SE SDK but are limited in their utility for all but the simplest types of problems. Other libraries such as Apache's OpenNLP and LingPipe provide extensive and sophisticated support for NLP problems.

Low-level Java support includes string libraries, such as `String`, `StringBuilder`, and `StringBuffer`. These classes possess methods that perform searching, matching, and text replacement. **Regular expressions** use special encoding to match substrings. Java provides a rich set of techniques to use regular expressions.

As discussed earlier, tokenizers are used to split text into individual elements. Java provides supports for tokenizers with:

- The `String` class' `split` method
- The `StreamTokenizer` class
- The `StringTokenizer` class

There also exists a number of NLP libraries/APIs for Java. A partial list of Java-based NLP APIs are found in the following table. Most of these are open source. In addition, there are a number of commercial APIs available. We will focus on the open source APIs:

API	URL
Apertium	`http://www.apertium.org/`
General Architecture for Text Engineering	`http://gate.ac.uk/`
Learning Based Java	`http://cogcomp.cs.illinois.edu/page/software_view/11`
LinguaStream	`http://www.linguastream.org/`
LingPipe	`http://alias-i.com/lingpipe/`
Mallet	`http://mallet.cs.umass.edu/`
MontyLingua	`http://web.media.mit.edu/~hugo/montylingua/`
Apache OpenNLP	`http://opennlp.apache.org/`
UIMA	`http://uima.apache.org/`
Stanford Parser	`http://nlp.stanford.edu/software`

Many of these NLP tasks are combined to form a **pipeline**. A pipeline consists of various NLP tasks, which are integrated into a series of steps to achieve some processing goal. Examples of frameworks that support pipelines are GATE and Apache UIMA.

In the next section, we will coverer several NLP APIs in more depth. A brief overview of their capabilities will be presented along with a list of useful links for each API.

Apache OpenNLP

The Apache OpenNLP project addresses common NLP tasks and will be used throughout this book. It consists of several components that perform specific tasks, permit models to be trained, and support for testing the models. The general approach, used by OpenNLP, is to instantiate a model that supports the task from a file and then executes methods against the model to perform a task.

For example, in the following sequence, we will tokenize a simple string. For this code to execute properly, it must handle the `FileNotFoundException` and `IOException` exceptions. We use a try-with-resource block to open a `FileInputStream` instance using the `en-token.bin` file. This file contains a model that has been trained using English text:

```
try (InputStream is = new FileInputStream(
        new File(getModelDir(), "en-token.bin"))){
    // Insert code to tokenize the text
} catch (FileNotFoundException ex) {
    ...
} catch (IOException ex) {
    ...
}
```

An instance of the `TokenizerModel` class is then created using this file inside the `try` block. Next, we create an instance of the `Tokenizer` class, as shown here:

```
TokenizerModel model = new TokenizerModel(is);
Tokenizer tokenizer = new TokenizerME(model);
```

The `tokenize` method is then applied, whose argument is the text to be tokenized. The method returns an array of `String` objects:

```
String tokens[] = tokenizer.tokenize("He lives at 1511 W."
  + "Randolph.");
```

A for-each statement displays the tokens as shown here. The open and close brackets are used to clearly identify the tokens:

```
for (String a : tokens) {
    System.out.print("[" + a + "] ");
}
System.out.println();
```

When we execute this, we will get output as shown here:

[He] [lives] [at] [1511] [W.] [Randolph] [.]

In this case, the tokenizer recognized that W. was an abbreviation and that the last period was a separate token demarking the end of the sentence.

We will use the OpenNLP API for many of the examples in this book. OpenNLP links are listed in the following table:

OpenNLP	Website
Home	https://opennlp.apache.org/
Documentation	https://opennlp.apache.org/documentation.html
Javadoc	http://nlp.stanford.edu/nlp/javadoc/javanlp/index.html
Download	https://opennlp.apache.org/cgi-bin/download.cgi
Wiki	https://cwiki.apache.org/confluence/display/OPENNLP/Index%3bjsessionid=32B408C73729ACCCDD071D9EC354FC54

Stanford NLP

The Stanford NLP Group conducts NLP research and provides tools for NLP tasks. The Stanford CoreNLP is one of these toolsets. In addition, there are other tool sets such as the Stanford Parser, Stanford POS tagger, and the Stanford Classifier. The Stanford tools support English and Chinese languages and basic NLP tasks, including tokenization and name entity recognition.

These tools are released under the full GPL but it does not allow them to be used in commercial applications, though a commercial license is available. The API is well organized and supports the core NLP functionality.

There are several tokenization approaches supported by the Stanford group. We will use the PTBTokenizer class to illustrate the use of this NLP library. The constructor demonstrated here uses a Reader object, a LexedTokenFactory<T> argument, and a string to specify which of the several options is to be used.

The `LexedTokenFactory` is an interface that is implemented by the `CoreLabelTokenFactory` and `WordTokenFactory` classes. The former class supports the retention of the beginning and ending character positions of a token, whereas the latter class simply returns a token as a string without any positional information. The `WordTokenFactory` class is used by default.

The `CoreLabelTokenFactory` class is used in the following example. A `StringReader` is created using a string. The last argument is used for the option parameter, which is `null` for this example. The `Iterator` interface is implemented by the `PTBTokenizer` class allowing us to use the `hasNext` and `next` methods to display the tokens:

```
PTBTokenizer ptb = new PTBTokenizer(
new StringReader("He lives at 1511 W. Randolph."),
new CoreLabelTokenFactory(), null);
while (ptb.hasNext()) {
  System.out.println(ptb.next());
}
```

The output is as follows:

```
He
lives
at
1511
W.
Randolph
.
```

We will use the Stanford NLP library extensively in this book. A list of Stanford links is found in the following table. Documentation and download links are found in each of the distributions:

Stanford NLP	Website
Home	`http://nlp.stanford.edu/index.shtml`
CoreNLP	`http://nlp.stanford.edu/software/corenlp.shtml#Download`
Parser	`http://nlp.stanford.edu/software/lex-parser.shtml`
POS Tagger	`http://nlp.stanford.edu/software/tagger.shtml`
java-nlp-user Mailing List	`https://mailman.stanford.edu/mailman/listinfo/java-nlp-user`

LingPipe

LingPipe consists of a set of tools to perform common NLP tasks. It supports model training and testing. There are both royalty free and license versions of the tool. The production use of the free version is limited.

To demonstrate the use of LingPipe, we will illustrate how it can be used to tokenize text using the `Tokenizer` class. Start by declaring two lists, one to hold the tokens and a second to hold the whitespace:

```
List<String> tokenList = new ArrayList<>();
List<String> whiteList = new ArrayList<>();
```

> **Downloading the example code**
>
> You can download the example code files for all Packt books you have purchased from your account at http://www.packtpub.com. If you purchased this book elsewhere, you can visit http://www.packtpub.com/support and register to have the files e-mailed directly to you.

Next, declare a string to hold the text to be tokenized:

```
String text = "A sample sentence processed \nby \tthe " +
    "LingPipe tokenizer.";
```

Now, create an instance of the `Tokenizer` class. As shown in the following code block, a static `tokenizer` method is used to create an instance of the `Tokenizer` class based on a `Indo-European factory` class:

```
Tokenizer tokenizer = IndoEuropeanTokenizerFactory.INSTANCE.
tokenizer(text.toCharArray(), 0, text.length());
```

The `tokenize` method of this class is then used to populate the two lists:

```
tokenizer.tokenize(tokenList, whiteList);
```

Use a for-each statement to display the tokens:

```
for(String element : tokenList) {
  System.out.print(element + " ");
}
System.out.println();
```

The output of this example is shown here:

`A sample sentence processed by the LingPipe tokenizer`

A list of LingPipe links can be found in the following table:

LingPipe	Website
Home	`http://alias-i.com/lingpipe/index.html`
Tutorials	`http://alias-i.com/lingpipe/demos/tutorial/read-me.html`
JavaDocs	`http://alias-i.com/lingpipe/docs/api/index.html`
Download	`http://alias-i.com/lingpipe/web/install.html`
Core	`http://alias-i.com/lingpipe/web/download.html`
Models	`http://alias-i.com/lingpipe/web/models.html`

GATE

General Architecture for Text Engineering (GATE) is a set of tools written in Java and developed at the University of Sheffield in England. It supports many NLP tasks and languages. It can also be used as a pipeline for NLP processing.

It supports an API along with GATE Developer, a document viewer that displays text along with annotations. This is useful for examining a document using highlighted annotations. GATE Mimir, a tool for indexing and searching text generated by various sources, is also available. Using GATE for many NLP tasks involves a bit of code. GATE Embedded is used to embed GATE functionality directly in code. Useful GATE links are listed in the following table:

Gate	Website
Home	`https://gate.ac.uk/`
Documentation	`https://gate.ac.uk/documentation.html`
JavaDocs	`http://jenkins.gate.ac.uk/job/GATE-Nightly/javadoc/`
Download	`https://gate.ac.uk/download/`
Wiki	`http://gatewiki.sf.net/`

UIMA

The **Organization for the Advancement of Structured Information Standards (OASIS)** is a consortium focused on information-oriented business technologies. It developed the **Unstructured Information Management Architecture (UIMA)** standard as a framework for NLP pipelines. It is supported by the Apache UIMA.

Although it supports pipeline creation, it also describes a series of design patterns, data representations, and user roles for the analysis of text. UIMA links are listed in the following table:

Apache UIMA	Website
Home	`https://uima.apache.org/`
Documentation	`https://uima.apache.org/documentation.html`
JavaDocs	`https://uima.apache.org/d/uimaj-2.6.0/apidocs/index.html`
Download	`https://uima.apache.org/downloads.cgi`
Wiki	`https://cwiki.apache.org/confluence/display/UIMA/Index`

Overview of text processing tasks

Although there are numerous NLP tasks that can be performed, we will focus only on a subset of these tasks. A brief overview of these tasks is presented here, which is also reflected in the following chapters:

- Finding Parts of Text
- Finding Sentences
- Finding People and Things
- Detecting Parts of Speech
- Classifying Text and Documents
- Extracting Relationships
- Combined Approaches

Many of these tasks are used together with other tasks to achieve some objective. We will see this as we progress through the book. For example, tokenization is frequently used as an initial step in many of the other tasks. It is a fundamental and basic step.

Finding parts of text

Text can be decomposed into a number of different types of elements such as words, sentences, and paragraphs. There are several ways of classifying these elements. When we refer to parts of text in this book, we are referring to words, sometimes called tokens. **Morphology** is the study of the structure of words. We will use a number of morphology terms in our exploration of NLP. However, there are many ways of classifying words including the following:

- **Simple words**: These are the common connotations of what a word means including the 17 words of this sentence.

- **Morphemes**: These are the smallest units of a word that is meaningful. For example, in the word "bounded", "bound" is considered to be a morpheme. Morphemes also include parts such as the suffix, "ed".

- **Prefix/Suffix**: This precedes or follows the root of a word. For example, in the word graduation, the "ation" is a suffix based on the word "graduate".

- **Synonyms**: This is a word that has the same meaning as another word. Words such as small and tiny can be recognized as synonyms. Addressing this issue requires word sense disambiguation.

- **Abbreviations**: These shorten the use of a word. Instead of using Mister Smith, we use Mr. Smith.

- **Acronyms**: These are used extensively in many fields including computer science. They use a combination of letters for phrases such as FORmula TRANslation for FORTRAN. They can be recursive such as GNU. Of course, the one we will continue to use is NLP.

- **Contractions**: We'll find these useful for commonly used combinations of words such as the first word of this sentence.

- **Numbers**: A specialized word that normally uses only digits. However, more complex versions can include a period and a special character to reflect scientific notation or numbers of a specific base.

Identifying these parts is useful for other NLP tasks. For example, to determine the boundaries of a sentence, it is necessary to break it apart and determine which elements terminate a sentence.

The process of breaking text apart is called tokenization. The result is a stream of tokens. The elements of the text that determine where elements should be split are called **Delimiters**. For most English text, whitespace is used as a delimiter. This type of a delimiter typically includes blanks, tabs, and new line characters.

Tokenization can be simple or complex. Here, we will demonstrate a simple tokenization using the `String` class' `split` method. First, declare a string to hold the text that is to be tokenized:

```
String text = "Mr. Smith went to 123 Washington avenue.";
```

The `split` method uses a regular expression argument to specify how the text should be split. In the next code sequence, its argument is the string \\s+. This specifies that one or more whitespaces be used as the delimiter:

```
String tokens[] = text.split("\\s+");
```

A for-each statement is used to display the resulting tokens:

```
for(String token : tokens) {
   System.out.println(token);
}
```

When executed, the output will appear as shown here:

```
Mr.
Smith
went
to
123
Washington
avenue.
```

In *Chapter 2, Finding Parts of Text*, we will explore the tokenization process in depth.

Finding sentences

We tend to think of the process of identifying sentences as a simple process. In English, we look for termination characters such as a period, question mark, or exclamation mark. However, as we will see in *Chapter 3, Finding Sentences*, this is not always that simple. Factors that make it more difficult to find the end of sentences include the use of embedded periods in such phrases as "Dr. Smith" or "204 SW. Park Street".

This process is also called **Sentence Boundary Disambiguation (SBD)**. This is a more significant problem in English than it is in languages such as Chinese or Japanese that have unambiguous sentence delimiters.

Identifying sentences is useful for a number of reasons. Some NLP tasks, such as POS tagging and entity extraction, work on individual sentences. Question-anwering applications also need to identify individual sentences. For these processes to work correctly, sentence boundaries must be determined correctly.

The following example demonstrates how sentences can be found using the Stanford DocumentPreprocessor class. This class will generate a list of sentences based on either simple text or an XML document. The class implements the Iterable interface allowing it to be easily used in a for-each statement.

Start by declaring a string containing the sentences, as shown here:

```
String paragraph = "The first sentence. The second sentence.";
```

Create a StringReader object based on the string. This class supports simple read type methods and is used as the argument of the DocumentPreprocessor constructor:

```
Reader reader = new StringReader(paragraph);
DocumentPreprocessor documentPreprocessor =
new DocumentPreprocessor(reader);
```

The DocumentPreprocessor object will now hold the sentences of the paragraph. In the next statement, a list of strings is created and is used to hold the sentences found:

```
List<String> sentenceList = new LinkedList<String>();
```

Each element of the documentPreprocessor object is then processed and consists of a list of the HasWord objects, as shown in the following block of code. The HasWord elements are objects that represent a word. An instance of StringBuilder is used to construct the sentence with each element of the hasWordList element being added to the list. When the sentence has been built, it is added to the sentenceList list:

```
for (List<HasWord> element : documentPreprocessor) {
   StringBuilder sentence = new StringBuilder();
   List<HasWord> hasWordList = element;
   for (HasWord token : hasWordList) {
       sentence.append(token).append(" ");
   }
   sentenceList.add(sentence.toString());
}
```

A for-each statement is then used to display the sentences:

```
for (String sentence : sentenceList) {
   System.out.println(sentence);
}
```

The output will appear as shown here:

```
The first sentence .
The second sentence .
```

The SBD process is covered in depth in *Chapter 3, Finding Sentences*.

Finding people and things

Search engines do a pretty good job of meeting the needs of most users. People frequently use a search engine to find the address of a business or movie show times. A word processor can perform a simple search to locate a specific word or phrase in a text. However, this task can get more complicated when we need to consider other factors such as whether synonyms should be used or if we are interested in finding things closely related to a topic.

For example, let's say we visit a website because we are interested in buying a new laptop. After all, who doesn't need a new laptop? When you go to the site, a search engine will be used to find laptops that possess the features you are looking for. The search is frequently conducted based on previous analysis of vendor information. This analysis often requires text to be processed in order to derive useful information that can eventually be presented to a customer.

The presentation may be in the form of facets. These are normally displayed on the left-hand side of a web page. For example, the facets for laptops might include categories such as an Ultrabook, Chromebook, or hard disk size. This is illustrated in the following figure, which is part of an Amazon web page:

Some searches can be very simple. For example, the `String` class and related classes have methods such as the `indexOf` and `lastIndexOf` methods that can find the occurrence of a `String` class. In the simple example that follows, the index of the occurrence of the target string is returned by the `indexOf` method:

```
String text = "Mr. Smith went to 123 Washington avenue.";
String target = "Washington";
int index = text.indexOf(target);
System.out.println(index);
```

The output of this sequence is shown here:

22

This approach is useful for only the simplest problems.

When text is searched, a common technique is to use a data structure called an inverted index. This process involves tokenizing the text and identifying terms of interest in the text along with their position. The terms and their positions are then stored in the inverted index. When a search is made for the term, it is looked up in the inverted index and the positional information is retrieved. This is faster than searching for the term in the document each time it is needed. This data structure is used frequently in databases, information retrieval systems, and search engines.

More sophisticated searches might involve responding to queries such as: "Where are good restaurants in Boston?" To answer this query we might need to perform entity recognition/resolution to identify the significant terms in the query, perform semantic analysis to determine the meaning of the query, search and then rank candidate responses.

To illustrate the process of finding names, we use a combination of a tokenizer and the OpenNLP `TokenNameFinderModel` class to find names in a text. Since this technique may throw an `IOException`, we will use a `try-catch` block to handle it. Declare this block and an array of strings holding the sentences, as shown here:

```
try {
    String[] sentences = {
        "Tim was a good neighbor. Perhaps not as good a Bob " +
        "Haywood, but still pretty good. Of course Mr. Adam " +
        "took the cake!"};
    // Insert code to find the names here
} catch (IOException ex) {
    ex.printStackTrace();
}
```

Before the sentences can be processed, we need to tokenize the text. Set up the tokenizer using the `Tokenizer` class, as shown here:

```
Tokenizer tokenizer = SimpleTokenizer.INSTANCE;
```

We will need to use a model to detect sentences. This is needed to avoid grouping terms that may span sentence boundaries. We will use the `TokenNameFinderModel` class based on the model found in the `en-ner-person.bin` file. An instance of `TokenNameFinderModel` is created from this file as follows:

```
TokenNameFinderModel model = new TokenNameFinderModel(
new File("C:\\OpenNLP Models", "en-ner-person.bin"));
```

The `NameFinderME` class will perform the actual task of finding the name. An instance of this class is created using the `TokenNameFinderModel` instance, as shown here:

```
NameFinderME finder = new NameFinderME(model);
```

Use a for-each statement to process each sentence as shown in the following code sequence. The `tokenize` method will split the sentence into tokens and the `find` method returns an array of `Span` objects. These objects store the starting and ending indexes for the names identified by the `find` method:

```
for (String sentence : sentences) {
    String[] tokens = tokenizer.tokenize(sentence);
    Span[] nameSpans = finder.find(tokens);
    System.out.println(Arrays.toString(
    Span.spansToStrings(nameSpans, tokens)));
}
```

When executed, it will generate the following output:

```
[Tim, Bob Haywood, Adam]
```

The primary focus of *Chapter 4, Finding People and Things*, is name recognition.

Detecting Parts of Speech

Another way of classifying the parts of text is at the sentence level. A sentence can be decomposed into individual words or combinations of words according to categories, such as nouns, verbs, adverbs, and prepositions. Most of us learned how to do this in school. We also learned not to end a sentence with a preposition contrary to what we did in the second sentence of this paragraph.

Detecting the **Parts of Speech (POS)** is useful in other tasks such as extracting relationships and determining the meaning of text. Determining these relationships is called **Parsing**. POS processing is useful for enhancing the quality of data sent to other elements of a pipeline.

The internals of a POS process can be complex. Fortunately, most of the complexity is hidden from us and encapsulated in classes and methods. We will use a couple of OpenNLP classes to illustrate this process. We will need a model to detect the POS. The POSModel class will be used and instanced using the model found in the en-pos-maxent.bin file, as shown here:

```
POSModel model = new POSModelLoader().load(
    new File("../OpenNLP Models/" "en-pos-maxent.bin"));
```

The POSTaggerME class is used to perform the actual tagging. Create an instance of this class based on the previous model as shown here:

```
POSTaggerME tagger = new POSTaggerME(model);
```

Next, declare a string containing the text to be processed:

```
String sentence = "POS processing is useful for enhancing the "
    + "quality of data sent to other elements of a pipeline.";
```

Here, we will use a whitespace tokenizer to tokenize the text:

```
String tokens[] = WhitespaceTokenizer.INSTANCE.tokenize(sentence);
```

The tag method is then used to find those parts of speech, which stored the results in an array of strings:

```
String[] tags = tagger.tag(tokens);
```

The tokens and their corresponding tags are then displayed:

```
for(int i=0; i<tokens.length; i++) {
    System.out.print(tokens[i] + "[" + tags[i] + "] ");
}
```

When executed, the following output will be produced:

```
POS[NNP] processing[NN] is[VBZ] useful[JJ] for[IN] enhancing[VBG] the[DT]
quality[NN] of[IN] data[NNS] sent[VBN] to[TO] other[JJ] elements[NNS]
of[IN] a[DT] pipeline.[NN]
```

Each token is followed by an abbreviation, contained within brackets, for its part of speech. For example, NNP means that it is a proper noun. These abbreviations will be covered in *Chapter 5, Detecting Parts of Speech*, which is devoted to exploring this topic in depth.

Classifying text and documents

Classification is concerned with assigning labels to information found in text or documents. These labels may or may not be known when the process occurs. When labels are known, the process is called **classification**. When the labels are unknown, the process is called **clustering**.

Also of interest in NLP is the process of categorization. This is the process of assigning some text element into one of the several possible groups. For example, military aircraft can be categorized as either fighter, bomber, surveillance, transport, or rescue.

Classifiers can be organized by the type of output they produce. This can be binary, which results in a yes/no output. This type is often used to support spam filters. Other types will result in multiple possible categories.

Classification is more of a process than many of the other NLP tasks. It involves the steps that we will discuss in *Understanding NLP models* later in the chapter. Due to the length of this process, we will not illustrate the process here. In *Chapter 6, Classifying Text and Documents*, we will investigate the classification process and provide a detailed example.

Extracting relationships

Relationship extraction identifies relationships that exist in text. For example, with the sentence "The meaning and purpose of life is plain to see", we know that the topic of the sentence is "The meaning and purpose of life". It is related to the last phrase that suggests that it is "plain to see".

Humans can do a pretty good job at determining how things are related to each other, at least at a high level. Determining deep relationships can be more difficult. Using a computer to extract relationships can also be challenging. However, computers can process large datasets to find relationships that would not be obvious to a human or that could not be done in a reasonable period of time.

There are numerous relationships possible. These include relationships such as where something is located, how two people are related to each other, what are the parts of a system, and who is in charge. Relationship extraction is useful for a number of tasks including building knowledge bases, performing analysis of trends, gathering intelligence, and performing product searches. Finding relationships is sometimes called **Text Analytics**.

There are several techniques that we can use to perform relationship extractions. These are covered in more detail in *Chapter 7, Using a Parser to Extract Relationships*. Here, we will illustrate one technique to identify relationships within a sentence using the Stanford NLP StanfordCoreNLP class. This class supports a pipeline where annotators are specified and applied to text. **Annotators** can be thought of as operations to be performed. When an instance of the class is created, the annotators are added using a Properties object found in the java.util package.

First, create an instance of the Properties class. Then assign the annotators as follows:

```
Properties properties = new Properties();
properties.put("annotators", "tokenize, ssplit, parse");
```

We used three annotators, which specify the operations to be performed. In this case, these are the minimum required to parse the text. The first one, tokenize, will tokenize the text. The ssplit annotator splits the tokens into sentences. The last annotator, parse, performs the syntactic analysis, parsing, of the text.

Next, create an instance of the StanfordCoreNLP class using the properties' reference variable:

```
StanfordCoreNLP pipeline = new StanfordCoreNLP(properties);
```

Next, an Annotation instance is created, which uses the text as its argument:

```
Annotation annotation = new Annotation(
    "The meaning and purpose of life is plain to see.");
```

Apply the annotate method against the pipeline object to process the annotation object. Finally, use the prettyPrint method to display the result of the processing:

```
pipeline.annotate(annotation);
pipeline.prettyPrint(annotation, System.out);
```

The output of this code is shown as follows:

```
Sentence #1 (11 tokens):
The meaning and purpose of life is plain to see.
```

[Text=The CharacterOffsetBegin=0 CharacterOffsetEnd=3 PartOfSpeech=DT]
[Text=meaning CharacterOffsetBegin=4 CharacterOffsetEnd=11
PartOfSpeech=NN] [Text=and CharacterOffsetBegin=12 CharacterOffsetEnd=15
PartOfSpeech=CC] [Text=purpose CharacterOffsetBegin=16
CharacterOffsetEnd=23 PartOfSpeech=NN] [Text=of CharacterOffsetBegin=24
CharacterOffsetEnd=26 PartOfSpeech=IN] [Text=life CharacterOffsetBegin=27
CharacterOffsetEnd=31 PartOfSpeech=NN] [Text=is CharacterOffsetBegin=32
CharacterOffsetEnd=34 PartOfSpeech=VBZ] [Text=plain
CharacterOffsetBegin=35 CharacterOffsetEnd=40 PartOfSpeech=JJ] [Text=to
CharacterOffsetBegin=41 CharacterOffsetEnd=43 PartOfSpeech=TO] [Text=see
CharacterOffsetBegin=44 CharacterOffsetEnd=47 PartOfSpeech=VB] [Text=.
CharacterOffsetBegin=47 CharacterOffsetEnd=48 PartOfSpeech=.]

```
(ROOT
  (S
    (NP
      (NP (DT The) (NN meaning)
        (CC and)
        (NN purpose))
      (PP (IN of)
        (NP (NN life))))
    (VP (VBZ is)
      (ADJP (JJ plain)
        (S
          (VP (TO to)
            (VP (VB see))))))
    (. .)))
```

root(ROOT-0, plain-8)

det(meaning-2, The-1)

nsubj(plain-8, meaning-2)

conj_and(meaning-2, purpose-4)

prep_of(meaning-2, life-6)

cop(plain-8, is-7)

aux(see-10, to-9)

xcomp(plain-8, see-10)

The first part of the output displays the text along with the tokens and POS. This is followed by a tree-like structure showing the organization of the sentence. The last part shows relationships between the elements at a grammatical level. Consider the following example:

```
prep_of(meaning-2, life-6)
```

This shows how the preposition, "of", is used to relate the words "meaning" and "life". This information is useful for many text simplification tasks.

Using combined approaches

As suggested earlier, NLP problems often involve using more than one basic NLP task. These are frequently combined in a pipeline to obtain the desired results. We saw one use of a pipeline in the previous section, *Extracting relationships*.

Most NLP solutions will use pipelines. We will provide several examples of pipelines in *Chapter 8, Combined Approaches*.

Understanding NLP models

Regardless of the NLP task being performed or the NLP tool set being used, there are several steps that they all have in common. In this section, we will present these steps. As you go through the chapters and techniques presented in this book, you will see these steps repeated with slight variations. Getting a good understanding of them now will ease the task of learning the techniques.

The basic steps include:

- Identifying the task
- Selecting a model
- Building and training the model
- Verifying the model
- Using the model

We will discuss each of these tasks in the following sections.

Identifying the task

It is important to understand the problem that needs to be solved. Based on this understanding, a solution can be devised that consists of a series of steps. Each of these steps will use an NLP task.

For example, suppose we want to answer a query such as "Who is the mayor of Paris?" We will need to parse the query into the POS, determine the nature of the question, the qualifying elements of the question, and eventually use a repository of knowledge, created using other NLP tasks, to answer the question.

Other problems may not be quite as involved. We might only need to break apart text into components so that the text can be associated with a category. For example, a vendor's product description may be analyzed to determine the potential product categories. The analysis of the description of a car would allow it to be placed into categories such as sedan, sports car, SUV, or compact.

Once you have an idea of what NLP tasks are available, you will be better able to match it with the problem you are trying to solve.

Selecting a model

Many of the tasks that we will examine are based on models. For example, if we need to split a document into sentences, we need an algorithm to do this. However, even the best sentence boundary detection techniques have problems doing this correctly every time. This has resulted in the development of models that examine the elements of text and then use this information to determine where sentence breaks occur.

The right model can be dependent on the nature of the text being processed. A model that does well for determining the end of sentences for historical documents might not work well when applied to medical text.

Many models have been created that we can use for the NLP task at hand. Based on the problem that needs to be solved, we can make informed decisions as to which model is the best. In some situations, we might need to train a new model. These decisions frequently involve trade-offs between accuracy and speed. Understanding the problem domain and the required quality of results permits us to select the appropriate model.

Building and training the model

Training a model is the process of executing an algorithm against a set of data, formulating the model, and then verifying the model. We may encounter situations where the text that needs to be processed is significantly different from what we have seen and used before. For example, using models trained using journalistic text might not work well when processing tweets. This may mean that the existing models will not work well with this new data. When this situation arises, we will need to train a new model.

To train a model, we will often use data that has been "marked up" in such a way that we know the correct answer. For example, if we are dealing with POS tagging, then the data will have POS elements (such as nouns and verbs) marked in the data. When the model is being trained, it will use this information to create the model. This dataset is called a **corpus**.

Verifying the model

Once the model has been created, we need to verify it against a sample set. The typical verification approach is to use a sample set where the correct responses are known. When the model is used with this data, we are able to compare its result to the known good results and assess the quality of the model. Often, only part of a corpus is used for training while the other part is used for verification.

Using the model

Using the model is simply applying the model to the problem at hand. The details are dependent on the model being used. This was illustrated in several of the earlier demonstrations, such as in the *Detecting Parts of Speech* section where we used the POS model as contained in the `en-pos-maxent.bin` file.

Preparing data

An important step in NLP is finding and preparing data for processing. This includes data for training purposes and the data that needs to be processed. There are several factors that need to be considered. Here, we will focus on the support Java provides for working with characters.

We need to consider how characters are represented. Although we will deal primarily with English text, other languages present unique problems. Not only are there differences in how a character can be encoded, the order in which text is read will vary. For example, Japanese orders its text in columns going from right to left.

There are also a number of possible encodings. These include ASCII, Latin, and Unicode to mention a few. A more complete list is found in the following table. Unicode, in particular, is a complex and extensive encoding scheme:

Encoding	Description
ASCII	A character encoding using 128 (0-127) values.
Latin	There are several Latin variations that uses 256 values. They include various combination of the umlaut, such as ţ, and other characters. Various versions of Latin have been introduced to address various Indo-European languages, such as Turkish and Esperanto.
Big5	A two-byte encoding to address the Chinese character set.
Unicode	There are three encodings for Unicode: UTF-8, UTF-16, and UTF-32. These use 1, 2, and 4 bytes, respectively. This encoding is able to represent all known languages in existence today, including newer languages such as Klingon and Elvish.

Java is capable of handling these encoding schemes. The `javac` executable's `-encoding` command-line option is used to specify the encoding scheme to use. In the following command line, the `Big5` encoding scheme is specified:

```
javac -encoding Big5
```

Character processing is supported using the primitive data type `char`, the `Character` class, and several other classes and interfaces as summarized in the following table:

Character type	Description
`char`	Primitive data type.
`Character`	Wrapper class for `char`.
`CharBuffer`	This class support a buffer of `char` providing methods for get/put characters or a sequence of characters operations.
`CharSequence`	An interface implemented by `CharBuffer`, `Segment`, `String`, `StringBuffer` and `StringBuilder`. It supports read-only access to a sequence of chars.

Java also provides a number of classes and interfaces to support strings. These are summarized in the following table. We will use these in many of our examples. The `String`, `StringBuffer`, and `StringBuilder` classes provide similar string processing capabilities but differ in whether they can be modified and whether they are thread-safe. The `CharacterIterator` interface and the `StringCharacterIterator` class provide techniques to traverse character sequences.

The `Segment` class represents a fragment of text.

Class/Interface	Description
String	An immutable string.
StringBuffer	Represents a modifiable string. It is thread-safe.
StringBuilder	Compatible with the `StringBuffer` class but is not thread-safe.
Segment	Represents a fragment of text in a character array. It provides rapid access to character data in an array.
CharacterIterator	Defines an iterator for text. It supports bidirectional traversal of text.
StringCharacterIterator	A class that implements the `CharacterIterator` interface for a `String`.

We also need to consider the file format if we are reading from a file. Often data is obtained from sources where the words are annotated. For example, if we use a web page as the source of text, we will find that it is marked up with HTML tags. These are not necessarily relevant to the analysis process and may need to be removed.

The **Multi-Purpose Internet Mail Extensions (MIME)** type is used to characterize the format used by a file. Common file types are listed in the following table. Either we need to explicitly remove or alter the markup found in a file or use specialized software to deal with it. Some of the NLP APIs provide tools to deal with specialized file formats.

File format	MIME type	Description
Text	plain/text	Simple text file
Office Type Document	application/msword application/vnd.oasis.opendocument.text	Microsoft Office Open Office
PDF	application/pdf	Adobe Portable Document Format
HTML	text/html	Web pages
XML	text/xml	eXtensible Markup Language
Database	Not applicable	Data can be in a number of different formats

Many of the NLP APIs assume that the data is clean. When it is not, it needs to be cleaned lest we get unreliable and misleading results.

Summary

In this chapter we introduced NLP and it uses. We found that it is used in many places to solve many different types of problems ranging from simple searches to sophisticated classification problems. The Java support for NLP in terms of core string support and advanced NLP libraries were presented. The basic NLP tasks were explained and illustrated using code. We also examined the process of training, verifying, and using models.

In this book, we will lay the foundation for using the basic NLP tasks using both simple and more sophisticated approaches. You may find that some problems require only simple approaches and when that is the case, knowing how to use the simple techniques may be more than adequate. In other situations, a more complex technique may be needed. In either case, you will be prepared to identify what tool is needed and be able to choose the appropriate technique for the task.

In the next chapter, we will examine the process of tokenization in depth and see how it can be used to find parts of text.

2
Finding Parts of Text

Finding parts of text is concerned with breaking text down into individual units called tokens, and optionally performing additional processing on these tokens. This additional processing can include stemming, lemmatization, stopword removal, synonym expansion, and converting text to lowercase.

We will demonstrate several tokenization techniques found in the standard Java distribution. These are included because sometimes this is all you may need to do the job. There may be no need to import NLP libraries in this situation. However, these techniques are limited. This is followed by a discussion of specific tokenizers or tokenization approaches supported by NLP APIs. These examples will provide a reference for how the tokenizers are used and the type of output they produce. This is followed by a simple comparison of the differences between the approaches.

There are many specialized tokenizers. For example, the Apache Lucene project supports tokenizers for various languages and specialized documents. The `WikipediaTokenizer` class is a tokenizer that handles Wikipedia-specific documents and the `ArabicAnalyzer` class handles Arabic text. It is not possible to illustrate all of these varying approaches here.

We will also examine how certain tokenizers can be trained to handle specialized text. This can be useful when a different form of text is encountered. It can often eliminate the need to write a new and specialized tokenizer.

Next, we will illustrate how some of these tokenizers can be used to support specific operations such as stemming, lemmatization, and stopword removal. POS can also be considered as a special instance of parts of text. However, this topic is investigated in *Chapter 5, Detecting Parts of Speech*.

Understanding the parts of text

There are a number of ways of categorizing parts of text. For example, we may be concerned with character-level issues such as punctuations with a possible need to ignore or expand contractions. At the word level, we may need to perform different operations such as:

- Identifying morphemes using stemming and/or lemmatization
- Expanding abbreviations and acronyms
- Isolating number units

We cannot always split words with punctuations because the punctuations are sometimes considered to be part of the word, such as the word "can't". We may also be concerned with grouping multiple words to form meaningful phrases. Sentence detection can also be a factor. We do not necessarily want to group words that cross sentence boundaries.

In this chapter, we are primarily concerned with the tokenization process and a few specialized techniques such as stemming. We will not attempt to show how they are used in other NLP tasks. Those efforts are reserved for later chapters.

What is tokenization?

Tokenization is the process of breaking text down into simpler units. For most text, we are concerned with isolating words. Tokens are split based on a set of delimiters. These delimiters are frequently whitespace characters. Whitespace in Java is defined by the `Character` class' `isWhitespace` method. These characters are listed in the following table. However, there may be a need at times to use a different set of delimiters. For example, different delimiters can be useful when whitespace delimiters obscure text breaks, such as paragraph boundaries, and detecting these text breaks is important.

Character	Meaning
Unicode space character	(space_separator, line_separator, or paragraph_separator)
\t	U+0009 horizontal tabulation
\n	U+000A line feed
\u000B	U+000B vertical tabulation
\f	U+000C form feed
\r	U+000D carriage return
\u001C	U+001C file separator
\u001D	U+001D group separator

Character	Meaning
\u001E	U+001E record separator
\u001F	U+001F unit separator

The tokenization process is complicated by a large number of factors such as:

- **Language**: Different languages present unique challenges. Whitespace is a commonly used delimiter but it will not be sufficient if we need to work with Chinese, where they are not used.

- **Text format**: Text is often stored or presented using different formats. How simple text is processed versus HTML or other markup techniques will complicate the tokenization process.

- **Stopwords**: Commonly used words might not be important for some NLP tasks such as general searches. These common words are called stopwords. Stopwords are sometimes removed when they do not contribute to the NLP task at hand. These can include words such as "a", "and", and "she".

- **Text expansion**: For acronyms and abbreviations, it is sometimes desirable to expand them so that postprocesses can produce better quality results. For example, if a search is interested in the word "machine", then knowing that IBM stands for International Business Machines can be useful.

- **Case**: The case of a word (upper or lower) may be significant in some situations. For example, the case of a word can help identify proper nouns. When identifying the parts of text, conversion to the same case can be useful in simplifying searches.

- **Stemming** and **lemmatization:** These processes will alter the words to get to their "roots".

Removing stopwords can save space in an index and make the indexing process faster. However, some search engines do not remove stopwords because they can be useful for certain queries. For example, when performing an exact match, removing stopwords will result in misses. Also, the NER task often depends on stopword inclusion. Recognizing that "Romeo and Juliet" is a play is dependent on the inclusion of the word "and".

There are many lists which define stopwords. Sometimes what constitutes a stopword is dependent on the problem domain. A list of stopwords can be found at http://www.ranks.nl/stopwords. It lists a few categories of English stopwords and stopwords for languages other than English. At http://www.textfixer.com/resources/common-english-words.txt, you will find a comma-separated formatted list of English stopwords.

A list of the top ten stopwords adapted from Stanford (`http://library.stanford.edu/blogs/digital-library-blog/2011/12/stopwords-searchworks-be-or-not-be`) are listed in the following table:

Stopword	Occurrences
the	7,578
of	6,582
and	4,106
in	2,298
a	1,137
to	1,033
for	695
on	685
an	289
with	231

We will focus on the techniques used to tokenize English text. This usually involves using whitespace or other delimiters to return a list of tokens.

 Parsing is closely related to tokenization. They are both concerned with identifying parts of text, but parsing is also concerned with identifying the parts of speech and their relationship to each other.

Uses of tokenizers

The output of tokenization can be used for simple tasks such as spell checkers and processing simple searches. It is also useful for various downstream NLP tasks such as identifying POS, sentence detection, and classification. Most of the chapters that follow will involve tasks that require tokenization.

Frequently, the tokenization process is just one step in a larger sequence of tasks. These steps involve the use of pipelines, as we will illustrate in *Using a pipeline* later in this chapter. This highlights the need for tokenizers that produce quality results for the downstream task. If the tokenizer does a poor job, then the downstream task will be adversely affected.

There are many different tokenizers and tokenization techniques available in Java. There are several core Java classes that were designed to support tokenization. Some of these are now outdated. There are also a number of NLP APIs designed to address both simple and complex tokenization problems. The next two sections will examine these approaches. First, we will see what the Java core classes have to offer, and then we will demonstrate a number of the NLP API tokenization libraries.

Simple Java tokenizers

There are several Java classes that support simple tokenization; some of them are as follows:

- Scanner
- String
- BreakIterator
- StreamTokenizer
- StringTokenizer

Although these classes provide limited support, it is useful to understand how they can be used. For some tasks, these classes will suffice. Why use a more difficult to understand and less efficient approach when a core Java class can do the job? We will cover each of these classes as they support the tokenization process.

The StreamTokenizer and StringTokenizer classes should not be used for new development. Instead, the String class' split method is usually a better choice. They have been included here in case you run across them and wonder whether they should be used or not.

Using the Scanner class

The Scanner class is used to read data from a text source. This might be standard input or it could be from a file. It provides a simple-to-use technique to support tokenization.

The Scanner class uses whitespace as the default delimiter. An instance of the Scanner class can be created using a number of different constructors. The constructor in the following sequence uses a simple string. The next method retrieves the next token from the input stream. The tokens are isolated from the string, stored into a list of strings, and then displayed:

```
Scanner scanner = new Scanner("Let's pause, and then "
    + " reflect.");
```

```
List<String> list = new ArrayList<>();
while(scanner.hasNext()) {
    String token = scanner.next();
    list.add(token);
}
for(String token : list) {
    System.out.println(token);
}
```

When executed, we get the following output:

```
Let's
pause,
and
then
reflect.
```

This simple implementation has several shortcomings. If we needed our contractions to be identified and possibly split, as demonstrated with the first token, then this implementation fails to do it. Also, the last word of the sentence was returned with a period attached to it.

Specifying the delimiter

If we are not happy with the default delimiter, there are several methods we can use to change its behavior. Several of these methods are summarized in the following table Reference source not found. This list is provided to give you an idea of what is possible.

Method	Effect
useLocale	Uses the locale to set the default delimiter matching
useDelimiter	Sets the delimiters based on a string or a pattern
useRadix	Specifies the radix to use when working with numbers
skip	Skips input matching a pattern and ignores the delimiters
findInLine	Finds the next occurrence of a pattern ignoring delimiters

Here, we will demonstrate the use of the useDelimiter method. If we use the following statement immediately before the while statement in the previous section's example, the only delimiters that will be used will be the blank space, apostrophe, and period.

```
scanner.useDelimiter("[ ,.]");
```

When executed, the following will be displayed. The blank line reflects the use of the comma delimiter. It has the undesirable effect of returning an empty string as a token in this example:

```
Let's
pause


and
then
reflect
```

This method uses a pattern as defined in a string. The open and close brackets are used to create a class of characters. This is a regular expression that matches those three characters. An explanation of Java patterns can be found at `http://docs.oracle.com/javase/8/docs/api/`. The delimiter list can be reset to whitespaces using the `reset` method.

Using the split method

We demonstrated the `String` class' `split` method in *Chapter 1, Introduction to NLP*. It is duplicated here for convenience:

```
String text = "Mr. Smith went to 123 Washington avenue.";
String tokens[] = text.split("\\s+");
for (String token : tokens) {
    System.out.println(token);
}
```

The output is as follows:

```
Mr.
Smith
went
to
123
Washington
avenue.
```

The `split` method also uses a regular expression. If we replace the text with the same string we used in the previous section, "Let's pause, and then reflect.", we will get the same output.

The `split` method has an overloaded version that uses an integer to specify how many times the regular expression pattern is applied to the target text. Using this parameter can stop the operation after the specified number of matches has been made.

The `Pattern` class also has a `split` method. It will split its argument based on the pattern used to create the `Pattern` object.

Using the BreakIterator class

Another approach for tokenization involves the use of the `BreakIterator` class. This class supports the location of integer boundaries for different units of text. In this section, we will illustrate how it can be used to find words.

The class has a single default constructor which is protected. We will use the static `getWordInstance` method to get an instance of the class. This method is overloaded with one version using a `Locale` object. The class possesses several methods to access boundaries as listed in the following table. It has one field, DONE, that is used to indicate that the last boundary has been found.

Method	Usage
`first`	Returns the first boundary of the text
`next`	Returns the next boundary following the current one
`previous`	Returns the boundary preceding the current one
`setText`	Associates a string with the `BreakIterator` instance

To demonstrate this class, we declare an instance of the `BreakIterator` class and a string to use with it:

```
BreakIterator wordIterator = BreakIterator.getWordInstance();
String text = "Let's pause, and then reflect.";
```

The text is then assigned to the instance and the first boundary is determined:

```
wordIterator.setText(text);
int boundary = wordIterator.first();
```

The loop that follows will store the beginning and ending boundary indexes for word breaks using the `begin` and `end` variables. The boundary values are integers. Each boundary pair and its associated text are displayed.

When the last boundary is found, the loop terminates:

```
while (boundary != BreakIterator.DONE) {
    int begin = boundary;
    System.out.print(boundary + "-");
    boundary = wordIterator.next();
    int end = boundary;
    if(end == BreakIterator.DONE) break;
    System.out.println(boundary + " ["
    + text.substring(begin, end) + "]");
}
```

The output follows where the brackets are used to clearly delineate the text:

```
0-5 [Let's]
5-6 [ ]
6-11 [pause]
11-12 [,]
12-13 [ ]
13-16 [and]
16-17 [ ]
17-21 [then]
21-22 [ ]
22-29 [reflect]
29-30 [.]
```

This technique does a fairly good job of identifying the basic tokens.

Using the StreamTokenizer class

The `StreamTokenizer` class, found in the `java.io` package, is designed to tokenize an input stream. It is an older class and is not as flexible as the `StringTokenizer` class discussed in the next section. An instance of the class is normally created based on a file and will tokenize the text found in the file. It can be constructed using a string.

The class uses a `nextToken` method to return the next token in the stream. The token returned is an integer. The value of the integer reflects the type of token returned. Based on the token type, the token can be handled in different ways.

The `StreamTokenizer` class fields are shown in the following table:

Field	Data Type	Meaning
nval	double	Contains a number if the current token is a number
sval	String	Contains the token if the current token is a word token
TT_EOF	static int	A constant for the end of the stream
TT_EOL	static int	A constant for the end of the line
TT_NUMBER	static int	The number of tokens read
TT_WORD	static int	A constant indicating a word token
ttype	int	The type of token read

In this example, a tokenizer is created followed by the declaration of the `isEOF` variable, which is used to terminate the loop. The `nextToken` method returns the token type. Based on the token type, numeric and string tokens are displayed:

```
try {
    StreamTokenizer tokenizer = new StreamTokenizer(
            newStringReader("Let's pause, and then reflect."));
    boolean isEOF = false;
    while (!isEOF) {
        int token = tokenizer.nextToken();
        switch (token) {
            case StreamTokenizer.TT_EOF:
                isEOF = true;
                break;
            case StreamTokenizer.TT_EOL:
                break;
            case StreamTokenizer.TT_WORD:
                System.out.println(tokenizer.sval);
                break;
            case StreamTokenizer.TT_NUMBER:
                System.out.println(tokenizer.nval);
                break;
            default:
                System.out.println((char) token);
        }
    }
} catch (IOException ex) {
    // Handle the exception
}
```

When executed, we get the following output:

```
Let
'
```

This is not what we would normally expect. The problem is that the tokenizer uses apostrophes (single quote character) and double quotes to denote quoted text. Since there is no corresponding match, it consumes the rest of the string.

We can use the `ordinaryChar` method to specify which characters should be treated as common characters. The single quote and comma characters are designated as ordinary characters here:

```
tokenizer.ordinaryChar('\'');
tokenizer.ordinaryChar(',');
```

When these statements are added to the previous code and executed, we get the following output:

```
Let

'

s

pause

'

and

then

reflect.
```

The apostrophe is not a problem now. These two characters are treated as delimiters and returned as tokens. There is also a `whitespaceChars` method available that specifies which characters are to be treated as whitespaces.

Using the StringTokenizer class

The `StringTokenizer` class is found in the `java.util` package. It provides more flexibility than the `StreamTokenizer` class and is designed to handle strings from any source. The class' constructor accepts the string to be tokenized as its parameter and uses the `nextToken` method to return the token. The `hasMoreTokens` method returns `true` if more tokens exist in the input stream. This is illustrated in the following sequence:

```
StringTokenizerst = new StringTokenizer("Let's pause, and "
    + "then reflect.");
while (st.hasMoreTokens()) {
    System.out.println(st.nextToken());
}
```

When executed, we get the following output:

```
Let's
pause,
and
then
reflect.
```

The constructor is overloaded, allowing the delimiters to be specified and whether the delimiters should be returned as a token.

Performance considerations with java core tokenization

When using these core Java tokenization approaches, it is worthwhile to briefly discuss how well they perform. Measuring performance can be tricky at times due to the various factors that can impact code execution. With that said, an interesting comparison of the performance of several Java core tokenization techniques is found at `http://stackoverflow.com/questions/5965767/performance-of-stringtokenizer-class-vs-split-method-in-java`. For the problem they were addressing, the `indexOf` method was fastest.

NLP tokenizer APIs

In this section, we will demonstrate several different tokenization techniques using the OpenNLP, Stanford, and LingPipe APIs. Although there are a number of other APIs available, we restricted the demonstration to these APIs. The examples will give you an idea of what techniques are available.

We will use a string called `paragraph` to illustrate these techniques. The string includes a new line break that may occur in real text in unexpected places. It is defined here:

```
private String paragraph = "Let's pause, \nand then +
    + "reflect.";
```

Using the OpenNLPTokenizer class

OpenNLP possesses a `Tokenizer` interface that is implemented by three classes: `SimpleTokenizer`, `TokenizerME`, and `WhitespaceTokenizer`. This interface supports two methods:

- `tokenize`: This is passed a string to tokenize and returns an array of tokens as strings.
- `tokenizePos`: This is passed a string and returns an array of `Span` objects. The `Span` class is used to specify the beginning and ending offsets of the tokens.

Each of these classes is demonstrated in the following sections.

Using the SimpleTokenizer class

As the name implies, the `SimpleTokenizer` class performs simple tokenization of text. The `INSTANCE` field is used to instantiate the class as shown in the following code sequence. The `tokenize` method is executed against the `paragraph` variable and the tokens are then displayed:

```
SimpleTokenizer simpleTokenizer = SimpleTokenizer.INSTANCE;
String tokens[] = simpleTokenizer.tokenize(paragraph);
for(String token : tokens) {
    System.out.println(token);
}
```

When executed, we get the following output:

```
Let
'
s
pause
,
and
then
reflect
.
```

Using this tokenizer, punctuation is returned as separate tokens.

Using the WhitespaceTokenizer class

As its name implies, this class uses whitespaces as delimiters. In the following code sequence, an instance of the tokenizer is created and the `tokenize` method is executed against it using `paragraph` as input. The for statement then displays the tokens:

```
String tokens[] =
WhitespaceTokenizer.INSTANCE.tokenize(paragraph);
for (String token : tokens) {
    System.out.println(token);
}
```

The output is as follows:

Let's

pause,

and

then

reflect.

Although this does not separate contractions and similar units of text, it can be useful for some applications. The class also possesses a `tokizePos` method that returns boundaries of the tokens.

Using the TokenizerME class

The `TokenizerME` class uses models created using **Maximum Entropy (maxent)** and a statistical model to perform tokenization. The maxent model is used to determine the relationship between data, in our case, text. Some text sources, such as various social media, are not well formatted and use a lot of slang and special symbols such as emoticons. A statistical tokenizer, such as the maxent model, improves the quality of the tokenization process.

> A detailed discussion of this model is not possible here due to its complexity. A good starting point for an interested reader can be found at http://en.wikipedia.org/w/index.php?title=Multinomial_logistic_regression&redirect=no.

A `TokenizerModel` class hides the model and is used to instantiate the tokenizer. The model must have been previously trained. In the next example, the tokenizer is instantiated using the model found in the `en-token.bin` file. This model has been trained to work with common English text.

The location of the model file is returned by the method `getModelDir`, which you will need to implement. The returned value is dependent on where the models are stored on your system. Many of these models can be found at `http://opennlp.sourceforge.net/models-1.5/`.

After the instance of a `FileInputStream` class is created, the input stream is used as the argument of the `TokenizerModel` constructor. The `tokenize` method will generate an array of strings. This is followed by code to display the tokens:

```
try {
    InputStream modelInputStream = new FileInputStream(
        new File(getModelDir(), "en-token.bin"));
    TokenizerModel model = new
        TokenizerModel(modelInputStream);
    Tokenizer tokenizer = new TokenizerME(model);
    String tokens[] = tokenizer.tokenize(paragraph);
    for (String token : tokens) {
        System.out.println(token);
    }
} catch (IOException ex) {
    // Handle the exception
}
```

The output is as follows:

```
Let

's

pause

,

and

then

reflect

.
```

Using the Stanford tokenizer

Tokenization is supported by several Stanford NLP API classes; a few of them are as follows:

- The `PTBTokenizer` class
- The `DocumentPreprocessor` class
- The `StanfordCoreNLP` class as a pipeline

Each of these examples will use the `paragraph` string as defined earlier.

Using the PTBTokenizer class

This tokenizer mimics the **Penn Treebank 3 (PTB)** tokenizer (http://www.cis. upenn.edu/~treebank/). It differs from PTB in terms of its options and its support for Unicode. The PTBTokenizer class supports several older constructors; however, it is suggested that the three-argument constructor be used. This constructor uses a Reader object, a LexedTokenFactory<T>argument, and a string to specify which of the several options to use.

The LexedTokenFactory interface is implemented by the CoreLabelTokenFactory and WordTokenFactory classes. The former class supports the retention of the beginning and ending character positions of a token whereas the latter class simply returns a token as a string without any positional information. The WordTokenFactory class is used by default. We will demonstrate the use of both classes.

The CoreLabelTokenFactory class is used in the following example. A StringReader instance is created using paragraph. The last argument is used for the options, which is null for this example. The Iterator interface is implemented by the PTBTokenizer class allowing us to use the hasNext and next method to display the tokens.

```
PTBTokenizer ptb = new PTBTokenizer(
    new StringReader(paragraph), new
CoreLabelTokenFactory(),null);
while (ptb.hasNext()) {
    System.out.println(ptb.next());
}
```

The output is as follows:

Let

's

pause

,

and

then

reflect

.

The same output can be obtained using the WordTokenFactory class, as shown here:

```
PTBTokenizerptb = new PTBTokenizer(
    new StringReader(paragraph), new WordTokenFactory(), null);
```

The power of the `CoreLabelTokenFactory` class is realized with the options parameter of the `PTBTokenizer` constructor. These options provide a means to control the behavior of the tokenizer. Options include such controls as how to handle quotes, how to map ellipses, and whether it should treat British English spellings or American English spellings. A list of options can be found at `http://nlp.stanford.edu/nlp/javadoc/javanlp/edu/stanford/nlp/process/PTBTokenizer.html`.

In the following code sequence, the `PTBTokenizer` object is created using the `CoreLabelTokenFactory` variable `ctf` along with an option of "invertible=true". This option allows us to obtain and use a `CoreLabel` object which will give us the beginning and ending position of each token:

```
CoreLabelTokenFactory ctf = new CoreLabelTokenFactory();
PTBTokenizer ptb = new PTBTokenizer(
    new StringReader(paragraph),ctf,"invertible=true");
while (ptb.hasNext()) {
    CoreLabel cl = (CoreLabel)ptb.next();
    System.out.println(cl.originalText() + " (" +
        cl.beginPosition() + "-" + cl.endPosition() + ")");
}
```

The output of this sequence is as follows. The numbers within the parentheses indicate the tokens' beginning and ending positions:

```
Let (0-3)
's (3-5)
pause (6-11)
, (11-12)
and (14-17)
then (18-22)
reflect (23-30)
. (30-31)
```

Using the DocumentPreprocessor class

The `DocumentPreprocessor` class tokenizes input from an input stream. In addition, it implements the `Iterable` interface making it easy to traverse the tokenized sequence. The tokenizer supports the tokenization of simple text and XML data.

To illustrate this process, we will use an instance of `StringReader` class that uses the `paragraph` string, as defined here:

```
Reader reader = new StringReader(paragraph);
```

An instance of the `DocumentPreprocessor` class is then instantiated:

```
DocumentPreprocessor documentPreprocessor =
        new DocumentPreprocessor(reader);
```

The `DocumentPreprocessor` class implements the `Iterable<java.util.List<HasWord>>` interface. The `HasWord` interface contains two methods that deal with words: a `setWord` and a `word` method. The latter method returns a word as a string. In the next code sequence, the `DocumentPreprocessor` class splits the input text into sentences which are stored as a `List<HasWord>`. An `Iterator` object is used to extract a sentence and then a for-each statement will display the tokens:

```
Iterator<List<HasWord>> it = documentPreprocessor.iterator();
while (it.hasNext()) {
    List<HasWord> sentence = it.next();
    for (HasWord token : sentence) {
        System.out.println(token);
    }
}
```

When executed, we get the following output:

```
Let
's
pause
,
and
then
reflect
.
```

Using a pipeline

Here, we will use the `StanfordCoreNLP` class as demonstrated in *Chapter 1, Introduction to NLP*. However, we use a simpler annotator string to tokenize the paragraph. As shown next, a `Properties` object is created and assigned the annotators `tokenize` and `ssplit`.

The `tokenize` annotator specifies that tokenization will occur and the `ssplit` annotation results in sentences being split:

```
Properties properties = new Properties();
properties.put("annotators", "tokenize, ssplit");
```

The StanfordCoreNLP class and the Annotation classes are created next:

```
StanfordCoreNLP pipeline = new StanfordCoreNLP(properties);
Annotation annotation = new Annotation(paragraph);
```

The annotate method is executed to tokenize the text and then the prettyPrint method will display the tokens:

```
pipeline.annotate(annotation);
pipeline.prettyPrint(annotation, System.out);
```

Various statistics are displayed followed by the tokens marked up with position information in the output, which is as follows:

```
Sentence #1 (8 tokens):

Let's pause,

and then reflect.

[Text=Let CharacterOffsetBegin=0 CharacterOffsetEnd=3] [Text='s
CharacterOffsetBegin=3 CharacterOffsetEnd=5] [Text=pause
CharacterOffsetBegin=6 CharacterOffsetEnd=11] [Text=,
CharacterOffsetBegin=11 CharacterOffsetEnd=12] [Text=and
CharacterOffsetBegin=14 CharacterOffsetEnd=17] [Text=then
CharacterOffsetBegin=18 CharacterOffsetEnd=22] [Text=reflect
CharacterOffsetBegin=23 CharacterOffsetEnd=30] [Text=.
CharacterOffsetBegin=30 CharacterOffsetEnd=31]
```

Using LingPipe tokenizers

LingPipe supports a number of tokenizers. In this section, we will illustrate the use of the IndoEuropeanTokenizerFactory class. In later sections, we will demonstrate other ways that LingPipe supports tokenization. Its INSTANCE field provides an instance of an Indo-European tokenizer. The tokenizer method returns an instance of a Tokenizer class based on the text to be processed, as shown here:

```
char text[] = paragraph.toCharArray();
TokenizerFactory tokenizerFactory =
IndoEuropeanTokenizerFactory.INSTANCE;
Tokenizer tokenizer = tokenizerFactory.tokenizer(text, 0,
text.length);
for (String token : tokenizer) {
    System.out.println(token);
}
```

The output is as follows:

```
Let

'

s

pause

,

and

then

reflect

.
```

These tokenizers support the tokenization of "normal" text. In the next section, we will demonstrate how a tokenizer can be trained to deal with unique text.

Training a tokenizer to find parts of text

Training a tokenizer is useful when we encounter text that is not handled well by standard tokenizers. Instead of writing a custom tokenizer, we can create a tokenizer model that can be used to perform the tokenization.

To demonstrate how such a model can be created, we will read training data from a file and then train a model using this data. The data is stored as a series of words separated by whitespace and <SPLIT> fields. This <SPLIT> field is used to provide further information about how tokens should be identified. They can help identify breaks between numbers, such as 23.6, and punctuation characters such as commas. The training data we will use is stored in the file training-data.train, and is shown here:

```
These fields are used to provide further information about how tokens
should be identified<SPLIT>.
They can help identify breaks between numbers<SPLIT>, such as
23.6<SPLIT>, punctuation characters such as commas<SPLIT>.
```

The data that we use does not represent unique text, but it does illustrate how to annotate text and the process used to train a model.

We will use the OpenNLP TokenizerME class' overloaded train method to create a model. The last two parameters require additional explanations. The maxent is used to determine the relationship between elements of text.

We can specify the number of features the model must address before it is included in the model. These features can be thought of as aspects of the model. Iterations refer to the number of times the training procedure will iterate when determining the model's parameters. Few of the TokenME class parameters are as follows:

Parameter	Usage
String	A code for the language used
ObjectStream<TokenSample>	An ObjectStream parameter containing the training data
boolean	If true, then alphanumeric data is ignored
int	Specifies how many times a feature is processed
int	The number of iterations used to train the maxent model

In the example that follows, we start by defining a BufferedOutputStream object that will be used to store the new model. Several of the methods used in the example will generate exceptions, which are handled in catch blocks:

```
BufferedOutputStream modelOutputStream = null;
try {
    ...
} catch (UnsupportedEncodingException ex) {
    // Handle the exception
} catch (IOException ex) {
    // Handle the exception
}
```

An instance of an ObjectStream class is created using the PlainTextByLineStream class. This uses the training file and the character encoding scheme as its constructor arguments. This is used to create a second ObjectStream instance of the TokenSample objects. These objects are text with token span information included:

```
ObjectStream<String> lineStream = new PlainTextByLineStream(
    new FileInputStream("training-data.train"), "UTF-8");
ObjectStream<TokenSample> sampleStream =
    new TokenSampleStream(lineStream);
```

The train method can now be used as shown in the following code. English is specified as the language. Alphanumeric information is ignored. The feature and iteration values are set to 5 and *100* respectively.

```
TokenizerModel model = TokenizerME.train(
    "en", sampleStream, true, 5, 100);
```

The parameters of the train method are given in detail in the following table:

Parameter	Meaning
Language code	A string specifying the natural language used
Samples	The sample text
Alphanumeric optimization	If `true`, then alphanumeric are skipped
Cutoff	The number of times a feature is processed
Iterations	The number of iterations performed to train the model

The next code sequence will create an output stream and then write the model out to the `mymodel.bin` file. The model is then ready to be used:

```
BufferedOutputStream modelOutputStream = new
BufferedOutputStream(
    new FileOutputStream(new File("mymodel.bin")));
model.serialize(modelOutputStream);
```

The details of the output will not be discussed here. However, it essentially chronicles the training process. The output of the sequence is as follows, but the last section has been abbreviated where most of the iterations steps have been deleted to save space:

```
Indexing events using cutoff of 5

Dropped event F:[p=2, s=3.6,, p1=2, p1_num, p2=bok, p1f1=23, f1=3, f1_
num, f2=., f2_eos, f12=3.]
Dropped event F:[p=23, s=.6,, p1=3, p1_num, p2=2, p2_num, p21=23,
p1f1=3., f1=., f1_eos, f2=6, f2_num, f12=.6]
Dropped event F:[p=23., s=6,, p1=., p1_eos, p2=3, p2_num, p21=3.,
p1f1=.6, f1=6, f1_num, f2=,, f12=6,]
   Computing event counts...  done. 27 events
   Indexing...  done.
Sorting and merging events... done. Reduced 23 events to 4.
Done indexing.
Incorporating indexed data for training...
done.
   Number of Event Tokens: 4
      Number of Outcomes: 2
   Number of Predicates: 4
...done.
Computing model parameters ...
Performing 100 iterations.
```

```
1:   ...loglikelihood=-15.942385152878742   0.8695652173913043
2:   ...loglikelihood=-9.223608340603953    0.8695652173913043
3:   ...loglikelihood=-8.222154969329086    0.8695652173913043
4:   ...loglikelihood=-7.885816898591612    0.8695652173913043
5:   ...loglikelihood=-7.674336804488621    0.8695652173913043
6:   ...loglikelihood=-7.494512270303332    0.8695652173913043
Dropped event T:[p=23.6, s=,, p1=6, p1_num, p2=., p2_eos, p21=.6,
p1f1=6,, f1=,, f2=bok]
7:   ...loglikelihood=-7.327098298508153    0.8695652173913043
8:   ...loglikelihood=-7.1676028756216965   0.8695652173913043
9:   ...loglikelihood=-7.014728408489079    0.8695652173913043

...

100:  ...loglikelihood=-2.3177060257465376   1.0
```

We can use the model as shown in the following sequence. This is the same technique we used in the section *Using the TokenizerME class*. The only difference is the model used here:

```java
try {
    paragraph = "A demonstration of how to train a
tokenizer.";
    InputStream modelIn = new FileInputStream(new File(
        ".", "mymodel.bin"));
    TokenizerModel model = new TokenizerModel(modelIn);
    Tokenizer tokenizer = new TokenizerME(model);
    String tokens[] = tokenizer.tokenize(paragraph);
    for (String token : tokens) {
        System.out.println(token);
    } catch (IOException ex) {
        ex.printStackTrace();
    }
}
```

The output is as follows:

```
A
demonstration
of
how
to
train
a
tokenizer
.
```

Comparing tokenizers

A brief comparison of the NLP APIs tokenizers is shown in the following table. The tokens generated are listed under the tokenizer's name. They are based on the same text, "Let's pause, \nand then reflect.". Keep in mind that the output is based on a simple use of the classes. There may be options not included in the examples that will influence how the tokens are generated. The intent is to simply show the type of output that can be expected based on the sample code and data.

Simple Tokenizer	Whitespace Tokenizer	Tokenizer ME	PTB Tokenizer	Document Preprocessor	IndoEuropean TokenizerFactory
Let	Let's	Let	Let	Let	Let
'	pause,	's	's	's	'
s	and	pause	pause	pause	s
pause	then	,	,	,	pause
,	reflect.	and	and	and	,
and		then	then	then	and
then		reflect	reflect	reflect	then
reflect		.	.	.	reflect
.					.

Understanding normalization

Normalization is a process that converts a list of words to a more uniform sequence. This is useful in preparing text for later processing. By transforming the words to a standard format, other operations are able to work with the data and will not have to deal with issues that might compromise the process. For example, converting all words to lowercase will simplify the searching process.

The normalization process can improve text matching. For example, there are several ways that the term "modem router" can be expressed, such as modem and router, modem & router, modem/router, and modem-router. By normalizing these words to the common form, it makes it easier to supply the right information to a shopper.

Understand that the normalization process might also compromise an NLP task. Converting to lowercase letters can decrease the reliability of searches when the case is important.

Normalization operations can include the following:

- Changing characters to lowercase
- Expanding abbreviations
- Removing stopwords
- Stemming and lemmatization

We will investigate these techniques here except for expanding abbreviations. This technique is similar to the technique used to remove stopwords, except that the abbreviations are replaced with their expanded version.

Converting to lowercase

Converting text to lowercase is a simple process that can improve search results. We can either use Java methods such as the `String` class' `toLowerCase` method, or use the capability found in some NLP APIs such as LingPipe's `LowerCaseTokenizerFactory` class. The `toLowerCase` method is demonstrated here:

```
String text = "A Sample string with acronyms, IBM, and UPPER "
   + "and lowercase letters.";
String result = text.toLowerCase();
System.out.println(result);
```

The output will be as follows:

```
a sample string with acronyms, ibm, and upper and lowercase letters.
```

LingPipe's `LowerCaseTokenizerFactory` approach is illustrated in the section *Normalizing using a pipeline*, later in this chapter.

Removing stopwords

There are several approaches to remove stopwords. A simple approach is to create a class to hold and remove stopwords. Also, several NLP APIs provide support for stopword removal. We will create a simple class called `StopWords` to demonstrate the first approach. We will then use LingPipe's `EnglishStopTokenizerFactory` class to demonstrate the second approach.

Creating a StopWords class

The process of removing stopwords involves examining a stream of tokens, comparing them to a list of stopwords, and then removing the stopwords from the stream. To illustrate this approach, we will create a simple class that supports basic operations as defined in the following table:

Constructor/Method	Usage
Default constructor	Uses a default set of stopwords
Single argument constructor	Uses stopwords stored in a file
addStopWord	Adds a new stopword to the internal list
removeStopWords	Accepts an array of words and returns a new array with the stopwords removed

Create a class called StopWords, which declares two instance variables as shown in the following code block. The variable defaultStopWords is an array that holds the default stopword list. The HashSet variable stopwords list is used to hold the stopwords for processing purposes:

```
public class StopWords {

    private String[] defaultStopWords = {"i", "a", "about", "an",
        "are", "as", "at", "be", "by", "com", "for", "from", "how",
        "in", "is", "it", "of", "on", "or", "that", "the", "this",
        "to", "was", "what", "when", where", "who", "will", "with"};

    private static HashSet stopWords  = new HashSet();
    ...
}
```

Two constructors of the class follow which populate the HashSet:

```
public StopWords() {
    stopWords.addAll(Arrays.asList(defaultStopWords));
}

public StopWords(String fileName) {
    try {
```

```
          BufferedReader bufferedreader =
                  new BufferedReader(new FileReader(fileName));
          while (bufferedreader.ready()) {
              stopWords.add(bufferedreader.readLine());
          }
      } catch (IOException ex) {
          ex.printStackTrace();
      }
  }
```

The convenience method `addStopWord` allows additional words to be added:

```
public void addStopWord(String word) {
    stopWords.add(word);
}
```

The `removeStopWords` method is used to remove the stopwords. It creates an `ArrayList` to hold the original words passed to the method. The for loop is used to remove stopwords from this list. The `contains` method will determine if the word submitted is a stopword, and if so, remove it. The `ArrayList` is converted to an array of strings and then returned. This is shown as follows:

```
public String[] removeStopWords(String[] words) {
    ArrayList<String> tokens =
        new ArrayList<String>(Arrays.asList(words));
    for (int i = 0; i < tokens.size(); i++) {
        if (stopWords.contains(tokens.get(i))) {
            tokens.remove(i);
        }
    }
    return (String[]) tokens.toArray(
        new String[tokens.size()]);
}
```

The following sequence illustrates how `StopWords` can be used. First, we declare an instance of the `StopWords` class using the default constructor. The OpenNLP `SimpleTokenizer` class is declared and the sample text is defined, as shown here:

```
StopWords stopWords = new StopWords();
SimpleTokenizer simpleTokenizer = SimpleTokenizer.INSTANCE;
paragraph = "A simple approach is to create a class "
    + "to hold and remove stopwords.";
```

The sample text is tokenized and then passed to the removeStopWords method. The new list is then displayed:

```
String tokens[] = simpleTokenizer.tokenize(paragraph);
String list[] = stopWords.removeStopWords(tokens);
for (String word : list) {
    System.out.println(word);
}
```

When executed, we get the following output. The "A" is not removed because it is uppercase and the class does not perform case conversion:

```
A
simple
approach
create
class
hold
remove
stopwords
.
```

Using LingPipe to remove stopwords

LingPipe possesses the EnglishStopTokenizerFactory class that we will use to identify and remove stopwords. The words in this list are found in http://alias-i.com/lingpipe/docs/api/com/aliasi/tokenizer/EnglishStopTokenizerFactory.html. They include words such as a, was, but, he, and for.

The factory class' constructor requires a TokenizerFactory instance as its argument. We will use the factory's tokenizer method to process a list of words and remove the stopwords. We start by declaring the string to be tokenized:

```
String paragraph = "A simple approach is to create a class "
    + "to hold and remove stopwords.";
```

Next, we create an instance of a TokenizerFactory based on the IndoEuropeanTokenizerFactory class. We then use that factory as the argument to create our EnglishStopTokenizerFactory instance:

```
TokenizerFactory factory =
IndoEuropeanTokenizerFactory.INSTANCE;
factory = new EnglishStopTokenizerFactory(factory);
```

Using the LingPipe `Tokenizer` class and the factory's `tokenizer` method, the text as declared in the `paragraph` variable is processed. The `tokenizer` method uses an array of `char`, a starting index, and its length:

```
Tokenizer tokenizer = factory.tokenizer(paragraph.toCharArray(),
    0, paragraph.length());
```

The following for-each statement will iterate over the revised list:

```
for (String token : tokenizer) {
    System.out.println(token);
}
```

The output will be as follows:

```
A
simple
approach
create
class
hold
remove
stopwords
.
```

Notice that although the letter, "A" is a stopword, it was not removed from the list. This is because the stopword list uses a lowercase 'a' and not an uppercase 'A'. As a result, it missed the word. We will correct this problem in the section *Normalizing using a pipeline*, later in the chapter.

Using stemming

Finding the stem of a word involves removing any prefixes or suffixes and what is left is considered to be the stem. Identifying stems is useful for tasks where finding similar words is important. For example, a search may be looking for occurrences of words like "book". There are many words that contain this word including books, booked, bookings, and bookmark. It can be useful to identify stems and then look for their occurrence in a document. In many situations, this can improve the quality of a search.

A stemmer may produce a stem that is not a real word. For example, it may decide that bounties, bounty, and bountiful all have the same stem, "bounti". This can still be useful for searches.

Similar to stemming is **Lemmatization**. This is the process of finding its **lemma**, its form as found in a dictionary. This can also be useful for some searches. Stemming is frequently viewed as a more primitive technique, where the attempt to get to the "root" of a word involves cutting off parts of the beginning and/or ending of a token.

Lemmatization can be thought of as a more sophisticated approach where effort is devoted to finding the morphological or vocabulary meaning of a token. For example, the word "having" has a stem of "hav" while its lemma is "have". Also, the words "was" and "been" have different stems but the same lemma, "be".

Lemmatization can often use more computational resources than stemming. They both have their place and their utility is partially determined by the problem that needs to be solved.

Using the Porter Stemmer

The **Porter Stemmer** is a commonly used stemmer for English. Its home page can be found at http://tartarus.org/martin/PorterStemmer/. It uses five steps to stem a word.

Although Apache OpenNLP 1.5.3 does not contain the PorterStemmer class, its source code can be downloaded from https://svn.apache.org/repos/asf/opennlp/trunk/opennlp-tools/src/main/java/opennlp/tools/stemmer/PorterStemmer.java. It can then be added to your project.

In the next example, we demonstrate the PorterStemmer class against an array of words. The input could as easily have originated from some other text source. An instance of the PorterStemmer class is created and then its stem method is applied to each word of the array:

```
String words[] = {"bank", "banking", "banks", "banker", "banked",
    "bankart"};
PorterStemmer ps = new PorterStemmer();
for(String word : words) {
    String stem = ps.stem(word);
    System.out.println("Word: " + word + "  Stem: " + stem);
}
```

When executed, you will get the following output:

Word: bank   Stem: bank

Word: banking   Stem: bank

```
Word: banks   Stem: bank
Word: banker  Stem: banker
Word: banked  Stem: bank
Word: bankart   Stem: bankart
```

The last word is used in combination with the word "lesion" as in "Bankart lesion". This is an injury of the shoulder and doesn't have much to do with the previous words. It does show that only common affixes are used when finding the stem.

Other potentially useful `PorterStemmer` class methods are found in the following table:

Method	Meaning
add	This will add a `char` to the end of the current stem word
stem	The method used without an argument will return `true` if a different stem occurs
reset	Reset the stemmer so a different word can be used

Stemming with LingPipe

The `PorterStemmerTokenizerFactory` class is used to find stems using LingPipe. In this example, we will use the same words array as in the previous section. The `IndoEuropeanTokenizerFactory` class is used to perform the initial tokenization followed by the use of the Porter Stemmer. These classes are defined here:

```
TokenizerFactory tokenizerFactory =
IndoEuropeanTokenizerFactory.INSTANCE;
TokenizerFactory porterFactory =
    new PorterStemmerTokenizerFactory(tokenizerFactory);
```

An array to hold the stems is declared next. We reuse the `words` array declared in the previous section. Each word is processed individually. The word is tokenized and its stem is stored in `stems` as shown in the following code block. The words and their stems are then displayed:

```
String[] stems = new String[words.length];
for (int i = 0; i < words.length; i++) {
    Tokenization tokenizer = new Tokenization(words[i],porterFactory);
    stems = tokenizer.tokens();
    System.out.print("Word: " + words[i]);
    for (String stem : stems) {
        System.out.println("  Stem: " + stem);
    }
}
```

When executed, we get the following output:

```
Word: bank   Stem: bank
Word: banking  Stem: bank
Word: banks  Stem: bank
Word: banker   Stem: banker
Word: banked   Stem: bank
Word: bankart  Stem: bankart
```

We have demonstrated Porter Stemmer using OpenNLP and LingPipe examples. It is worth noting that there are other types of stemmers available including NGrams and various mixed probabilistic/algorithmic approaches.

Using lemmatization

Lemmatization is supported by a number of NLP APIs. In this section, we will illustrate how lemmatization can be performed using the StanfordCoreNLP and the OpenNLPLemmatizer classes. The lemmatization process determines the lemma of a word. A lemma can be thought of as the dictionary form of a word. For example, the lemma of "was" is "be".

Using the StanfordLemmatizer class

We will use the StanfordCoreNLP class with a pipeline to demonstrate lemmatization. We start by setting up the pipeline with four annotators including lemma as shown here:

```
StanfordCoreNLP pipeline;
Properties props = new Properties();
props.put("annotators", "tokenize, ssplit, pos, lemma");
pipeline = new StanfordCoreNLP(props);
```

These annotators are needed and are explained as follows:

Annotator	Operation to be Performed
tokenize	Tokenization
ssplit	Sentence splitting
pos	POS tagging
lemma	Lemmatization
ner	NER

Annotator	Operation to be Performed
parse	Syntactic parsing
dcoref	Coreference resolution

A paragraph variable is used with the Annotation constructor and the annotate method is then executed, as shown here:

```
String paragraph = "Similar to stemming is Lemmatization. "
    +"This is the process of finding its lemma, its form " +
    +"as found in a dictionary.";
Annotation document = new Annotation(paragraph);
pipeline.annotate(document);
```

We now need to iterate over the sentences and tokens of the sentences. The Annotation and CoreMap class' get methods will return values of the type specified. If there are no values of the specified type, it will return null. We will use these classes to obtain a list of lemmas.

First, a list of sentences is returned and then each word of each sentence is processed to find lemmas. The list of sentences and lemmas are declared here:

```
List<CoreMap> sentences =
    document.get(SentencesAnnotation.class);
List<String> lemmas = new LinkedList<>();
```

Two for-each statements iterate over the sentences to populate the lemmas list. Once this is completed, the list is displayed:

```
for (CoreMap sentence : sentences) {
    for (CoreLabelword : sentence.get(TokensAnnotation.class)) {
        lemmas.add(word.get(LemmaAnnotation.class));
    }
}

System.out.print("[");
for (String element : lemmas) {
    System.out.print(element + " ");
}
System.out.println("]");
```

The output of this sequence is as follows:

```
[similar to stem be lemmatization . this be the process of find its lemma
, its form as find in a dictionary . ]
```

Comparing this to the original test, we see that it does a pretty good job:

```
Similar to stemming is Lemmatization. This is the process of finding its
lemma, its form as found in a dictionary.
```

Using lemmatization in OpenNLP

OpenNLP also supports lemmatization using the JWNLDictionary class. This class' constructor uses a string that contains the path of the dictionary files used to identify roots. We will use a WordNet dictionary developed at Princeton University (wordnet.princeton.edu). The actual dictionary is a series of files stored in a directory. These files contain a list of words and their "root". For the example used in this section, we will use the dictionary found at https://code.google.com/p/ xssm/downloads/detail?name=SimilarityUtils.zip&can=2&q=.

The JWNLDictionary class' getLemmas method is passed the word we want to process and a second parameter that specifies the POS for the word. It is important that the POS match the actual word type if we want accurate results.

In the next code sequence, we create an instance of the JWNLDictionary class using a path ending with \\dict\\. This is the location of the dictionary. We also define our sample text. The constructor can throw IOException and JWNLException, which we deal with in a try-catch block sequence:

```
try {
    dictionary = new JWNLDictionary("…\\dict\\");
    paragraph = "Eat, drink, and be merry, for life is but a dream";
    …
} catch (IOException | JWNLException ex)
    //
}
```

Following the text initialization, add the following statements. First, we tokenize the string using the WhitespaceTokenizer class as explained in the section *Using the WhitespaceTokenizer class*. Then, each token is passed to the getLemmas method with an empty string as the POS type. The original token and its lemmas are then displayed:

```
String tokens[] =
    WhitespaceTokenizer.INSTANCE.tokenize(paragraph);
for (String token : tokens) {
    String[] lemmas = dictionary.getLemmas(token, "");
    for (String lemma : lemmas) {
```

```
System.out.println("Token: " + token + "  Lemma: "
    + lemma);
    }
}
```

The output is as follows:

```
Token: Eat,   Lemma: at
Token: drink,   Lemma: drink
Token: be   Lemma: be
Token: life   Lemma: life
Token: is   Lemma: is
Token: is   Lemma: i
Token: a   Lemma: a
Token: dream   Lemma: dream
```

The lemmatization process works well except for the token "is" that returns two lemmas. The second one is not valid. This illustrates the importance of using the proper POS for a token. We could have used one or more of the POS tags as the argument to the getLemmas method. However, this begs the question: how do we determine the correct POS? This topic is discussed in detail in *Chapter 5, Detecting Parts of Speech.*

A short list of POS tags is found in the following table. This list is adapted from https://www.ling.upenn.edu/courses/Fall_2003/ling001/penn_treebank_pos.html. The complete list of The University of Pennsylvania (Penn) Treebank Tagset can be found at http://www.comp.leeds.ac.uk/ccalas/tagsets/upenn.html.

Tag	Description
JJ	Adjective
NN	Noun, singular or mass
NNS	Noun, plural
NNP	Proper noun, singular
NNPS	Proper noun, plural
POS	Possessive ending
PRP	Personal pronoun
RB	Adverb
RP	Particle
VB	Verb, base form
VBD	Verb, past tense
VBG	Verb, gerund or present participle

Normalizing using a pipeline

In this section, we will combine many of the normalization techniques using a pipeline. To demonstrate this process, we will expand upon the example used in *Using LingPipe* to remove stopwords. We will add two additional factories to normalize text: LowerCaseTokenizerFactory and PorterStemmerTokenizerFactory.

The LowerCaseTokenizerFactory factory is added before the creation of the EnglishStopTokenizerFactory and the PorterStemmerTokenizerFactory after the creation of the EnglishStopTokenizerFactory, as shown here:

```
paragraph = "A simple approach is to create a class "
    + "to hold and remove stopwords.";
TokenizerFactory factory =
    IndoEuropeanTokenizerFactory.INSTANCE;
factory = new LowerCaseTokenizerFactory(factory);
factory = new EnglishStopTokenizerFactory(factory);
factory = new PorterStemmerTokenizerFactory(factory);
Tokenizer tokenizer =
    factory.tokenizer(paragraph.toCharArray(), 0,
    paragraph.length());
for (String token : tokenizer) {
    System.out.println(token);
}
```

The output is as follows:

```
simpl

approach

creat

class

hold

remov

stopword

.
```

What we have left are the stems of the words in lowercase with the stopwords removed.

Summary

In this chapter, we illustrated various approaches to tokenize text and perform normalization on text. We started with simple tokenization technique based on core Java classes such as the `String` class' `split` method and the `StringTokenizer` class. These approaches can be useful when we decide to forgo the use of NLP API classes.

We demonstrated how tokenization can be performed using the OpenNLP, Stanford, and LingPipe APIs. We found there are variations in how tokenization can be performed and in options that can be applied in these APIs. A brief comparison of their outputs was provided.

Normalization was discussed, which can involve converting characters to lowercase, expanding abbreviation, removing stopwords, stemming, and lemmatization. We illustrated how these techniques can be applied using both core Java classes and the NLP APIs.

In the next chapter, we will investigate the issues involved with determining the end of sentences using various NLP APIs.

3
Finding Sentences

Partitioning text into sentences is also called **Sentence Boundary Disambiguation (SBD)**. This process is useful for many downstream NLP tasks that require analysis within sentences; for example, POS and phrase analysis typically work within a sentence.

In this chapter, we will explain in further detail why SBD is difficult. Then we will examine some core Java approaches that may work in some situations, and move on to the use of models by various NLP APIs. We will also examine training and validating approaches for sentence detection models. We can add additional rules to refine the process further, but this will work only up to a certain point. After that, models must be trained to handle both common and specialized situations. The later part of this chapter focuses on these models and their use.

The SBD process

The SBD process is language dependent and is often not straightforward. Common approaches to detect sentences include using a set of rules or training a model to detect them. A set of simple rules for detecting a sentence follows. The end of a sentence is detected if:

- The text is terminated by a period, question mark, or exclamation mark
- The period is not preceded by an abbreviation or followed by a digit

Although this works well for most sentences, it will not work for all of them. For example, it is not always easy to determine what an abbreviation is, and sequences such as ellipses may be confused with periods.

Most search engines are not concerned with SBD. They are only interested in a query's tokens and their positions. POS taggers and other NLP tasks that perform extraction of data will frequently process individual sentences. The detection of sentence boundaries will help separate phrases that might appear to span sentences. For example, consider the following sentence:

"The construction process was over. The hill where the house was built was short."

If we were searching for the phrase "over the hill", we would inadvertently pick up it here.

Many of the examples in this chapter will use the following text to demonstrate SBD. This text consists of three simple sentences followed by a more complicated sentence:

```
private static String paragraph = "When determining the end of sentences "
        + "we need to consider several factors. Sentences may end with "
        + "exclamation marks! Or possibly questions marks? Within "
        + "sentences we may find numbers like 3.14159, abbreviations "
        + "such as found in Mr. Smith, and possibly ellipses either "
        + "within a sentence …, or at the end of a sentence…";
```

What makes SBD difficult?

Breaking text into sentences is difficult for a number of reasons:

- Punctuation is frequently ambiguous
- Abbreviations often contain periods
- Sentences may be embedded within each other by the use of quotes
- With more specialized text, such as tweets and chat sessions, we may need to consider the use of new lines or completion of clauses

Punctuation ambiguity is best illustrated by the period. It is frequently used to demark the end of a sentence. However, it can be used in a number of other contexts as well, including abbreviation, numbers, e-mail addresses, and ellipses. Other punctuation characters, such as question and exclamation marks, are also used in embedded quotes and specialized text such as code that may be in a document.

Periods are used in a number of situations:

- To terminate a sentence
- To end an abbreviation
- To end an abbreviation and terminate a sentence
- For ellipses
- For ellipses at the end of a sentence
- Embedded in quotes or brackets

Most sentences we encounter end with a period. This makes them easy to identify. However, when they end with an abbreviation, it a bit more difficult to identify them. The following sentence contains abbreviations with periods:

"Mr. and Mrs. Smith went to the ball."

In the next two sentences, we have an abbreviation that occurs at the end of the sentence:

"He was an agent of the CIA."

"He was an agent of the C.I.A."

In the last sentence, each letter of the abbreviation is followed by a period. Although not common, this may occur and we cannot simply ignore it.

Another issue that makes SBD difficult is trying to determine whether or not a word is an abbreviation. We cannot simply treat all uppercase sequences as abbreviations. Perhaps the user typed in a word in all caps by accident or the text was preprocessed to convert all characters to lowercase. Also, some abbreviations consist of a sequence of uppercase and lowercase letters. To handle abbreviations, a list of valid abbreviations is sometimes used. However, the abbreviations are often domain-specific.

Ellipses can further complicate the problem. They may be found as a single character (Extended ASCII 0x85 or Unicode (U+2026)) or as a sequence of three periods. In addition, there is the Unicode horizontal ellipsis (U+2026), the vertical ellipsis (U+22EE), and the presentation form for the vertical and horizontal ellipsis (U+FE19). Besides these, there are HTML encodings. For Java, \uFE19 is used. These variations on encoding illustrate the need for good preprocessing of text before it is analyzed.

The next two sentences illustrate possible uses of the ellipses:

"And then there was … one."

"And the list goes on and on and …"

The second sentence was terminated by an ellipsis. In some situations, as suggested by the MLA handbook (`http://www.mlahandbook.org/fragment/public_index`), we can use brackets to distinguish ellipses that have been added from ellipses that were part of the original text, as shown here:

"The people [...] used various forms of transportation [...]" (*Young 73*).

We will also find sentences embedded in another sentence, such as:

The man said, "That's not right."

Exclamation marks and questions marks present other problems, even though the occurrence of these characters is more limited than that of the period. There are places other than at the end of a sentence where exclamation marks can occur. In the case of some words, such as Yahoo!, the exclamation mark is a part of the word. In addition, multiple exclamation marks are used for emphasis such as "Best wishes!!" This can lead to identification of multiple sentences where they do not actually exist.

Understanding SBD rules of LingPipe's HeuristicSentenceModel class

There are other rules that can be used to perform SBD. LingPipe's `HeuristicSentenceModel` class uses a series of token rules to perform SBD. We will present them here, as they provide insight into what rules can be useful.

This class uses three sets of tokens and two flags to assist in the process:

- **Possible Stops**: This is a set of tokens that can be the last token of a sentence
- **Impossible Penultimates**: These tokens cannot be the second to last token in a sentence
- **Impossible Starts**: This is a set of tokens that cannot be used to start a sentence
- **Balance Parentheses**: This flag indicates that a sentence should not be terminated until all matching parentheses are matched in that sentence
- **Force Final Boundary**: This specifies that the final token in an input stream should be treated as a sentence terminator even if it is not a possible stop

Balance parentheses include () and []. However, this rule will fail if the text is malformed. The default token sets are listed in the following table:

Possible Stops	Impossible Penultimates	Impossible Starts
.	any single letter	closed parentheses
..	personal and professional titles, ranks, and so on	,
!	commas, colons, and quotes	;
?	common abbreviations	:
"	directions	-
"	corporate designators	--
).	time, months, and so on	---
	U.S. political parties	%
	U.S. states (not ME or IN)	"
	shipping terms	
	address abbreviations	

Although LingPipe's `HeuristicSentenceModel` class uses these rules, there is no reason they cannot be used in other implementations of SBD tools.

Heuristic approaches for SBD might not always be as accurate as other techniques. However, they may work in a particular domain and often have the advantages of being faster and using less memory.

Simple Java SBDs

Sometimes, text may be simple enough that Java core support will suffice. There are two approaches that will perform SBD: using regular expressions and using the `BreakIterator` class. We will examine both approaches here.

Using regular expressions

Regular expressions can be difficult to understand. While simple expressions are not usually a problem, as they become more complex, their readability worsens. This is one of the limitations of regular expressions when trying to use them for SBD.

We will present two different regular expressions. The first expression is simple, but does not do a very good job. It illustrates a solution that may be too simple for some problem domains. The second is more sophisticated and does a better job.

In this example, we create a regular expression class that matches periods, question marks, and exclamation marks. The `String` class' `split` method is used to split the text into sentences:

```
String simple = "[.?!]";
String[] splitString = (paragraph.split(simple));
for (String string : splitString) {
    System.out.println(string);
}
```

The output is as follows:

```
When determining the end of sentences we need to consider several factors

 Sentences may end with exclamation marks

 Or possibly questions marks

 Within sentences we may find numbers like 3

14159, abbreviations such as found in Mr

 Smith, and possibly ellipses either within a sentence …, or at the end
of a sentence…
```

As expected, the method splits the paragraph into characters regardless of whether they are part of a number or abbreviation.

A second approach follows, which produces better results. This example has been adapted from an example found at `http://stackoverflow.com/questions/5553410/regular-expression-match-a-sentence`. The `Pattern` class, which compiles the following regular expression, is used:

`[^.!?\s] [^.!?]*(?:[.!?] (?![' "]?\s|$) [^.!?]*)*[.!?]?[' "]?(?=\s|$)`

The comment in the following code sequence provides an explanation of what each part represents:

```
Pattern sentencePattern = Pattern.compile(
    "# Match a sentence ending in punctuation or EOS.\n"
    + "[^.!?\\s]    # First char is non-punct, non-ws\n"
    + "[^.!?]*     # Greedily consume up to punctuation.\n"
    + "(?:         # Group for unrolling the loop.\n"
    + "  [.!?]     # (special) inner punctuation ok if\n"
    + "  (?![' \"]?\\s|$)  # not followed by ws or EOS.\n"
    + "  [^.!?]*   # Greedily consume up to punctuation.\n"
    + ")*          # Zero or more (special normal*)\n"
    + "[.!?]?      # Optional ending punctuation.\n"
    + "[' \"]?      # Optional closing quote.\n"
    + "(?=\\s|$)",
    Pattern.MULTILINE | Pattern.COMMENTS);
```

Another representation of this expression can be generated using the display tool found at `http://regexper.com/`. As shown in the following diagram, it graphically depicts the expression and can clarify how it works:

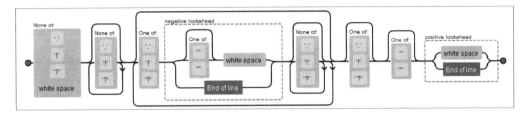

The `matcher` method is executed against the sample paragraph and then the results are displayed:

```
Matcher matcher = sentencePattern.matcher(paragraph);
while (matcher.find()) {
    System.out.println(matcher.group());
}
```

The output follows. The sentence terminators are retained, but there are still problems with abbreviations:

When determining the end of sentences we need to consider several factors.

Sentences may end with exclamation marks!

Or possibly questions marks?

Within sentences we may find numbers like 3.14159, abbreviations such as found in Mr.

Smith, and possibly ellipses either within a sentence …, or at the end of a sentence…

Using the BreakIterator class

The `BreakIterator` class can be used to detect various text boundaries such as those between characters, words, sentences, and lines. Different methods are used to create different instances of the `BreakIterator` class as follows:

- For characters, the `getCharacterInstance` method is used
- For words, the `getWordInstance` method is used
- For sentences, the `getSentenceInstance` method is used
- For lines, the `getLineInstance` method is used

Detecting breaks between characters is important at times, for example, when we need to process characters that are composed of multiple Unicode characters such as ü. This character is sometimes formed by combining the \u0075 (u) and \u00a8 (¨) Unicode characters. The class will identify these types of characters. This capability is further detailed at https://docs.oracle.com/javase/tutorial/i18n/text/char.html.

The BreakIterator class can be used to detect the end of a sentence. It uses a cursor that references the current boundary. It supports a next and a previous method that moves the cursor forward and backwards in the text, respectively. BreakIterator has a single, protected default constructor. To obtain an instance of the BreakIterator class to detect the end of a sentence, use the static getSentenceInstance method, as shown here:

```
BreakIterator sentenceIterator =
BreakIterator.getSentenceInstance();
```

There is also an overloaded version of the method. It takes a Locale instance as an argument:

```
Locale currentLocale = new Locale("en", "US");
BreakIterator sentenceIterator =
    BreakIterator.getSentenceInstance(currentLocale);
```

Once an instance has been created, the setText method will associate the text to be processed with the iterator:

```
sentenceIterator.setText(paragraph);
```

BreakIterator identifies the boundaries found in text using a series of methods and fields. All of these return integer values, and they are detailed in the following table:

Method	Usage
first	Returns the first boundary of the text
next	Returns the boundary following the current boundary
previous	Returns the boundary preceding the current boundary
DONE	The final integer, which is assigned a value of -1 (indicating that there are no more boundaries to be found)

To use the iterator in a sequential fashion, the first boundary is identified using the `first` method, and then the `next` method is called repeatedly to find the subsequent boundaries. The process is terminated when `Done` is returned. This technique is illustrated in the next code sequence, which uses the previously declared `sentenceIterator` instance:

```
int boundary = sentenceIterator.first();
while (boundary != BreakIterator.DONE) {
    int begin = boundary;
    System.out.print(boundary + "-");
    boundary = sentenceIterator.next();
    int end = boundary;
    if (end == BreakIterator.DONE) {
        break;
    }
    System.out.println(boundary + " ["
        + paragraph.substring(begin, end) + "]");
}
```

On execution, we get the following output:

```
0-75 [When determining the end of sentences we need to consider several
factors. ]

75-117 [Sentences may end with exclamation marks! ]

117-146 [Or possibly questions marks? ]

146-233 [Within sentences we may find numbers like 3.14159 ,
abbreviations such as found in Mr. ]

233-319 [Smith, and possibly ellipses either within a sentence … , or at
the end of a sentence…]

319-
```

This output works for simple sentences but is not successful with more complex sentences.

The uses of both regular expressions and the `BreakIterator` class have limitations. They are useful for text consisting of relatively simple sentences. However, when the text becomes more complex, it is better to use the NLP APIs instead, as discussed in the next section.

Using NLP APIs

There are a number of NLP API classes that support SBD. Some are rule-based, whereas others use models that have been trained using common and uncommon text. We will illustrate the use of sentence detection classes using the OpenNLP, Stanford, and LingPipe APIs.

The models can also be trained. The discussion of this approach is illustrated in the *Training a Sentence Detector model* section of this chapter. Specialized models are needed when working with specialized text such as medical or legal text.

Using OpenNLP

OpenNLP uses models to perform SBD. An instance of the SentenceDetectorME class is created, based on a model file. Sentences are returned by the sentDetect method, and position information is returned by the sentPosDetect method.

Using the SentenceDetectorME class

A model is loaded from a file using the SentenceModel class. An instance of the SentenceDetectorME class is then created using the model, and the sentDetect method is invoked to perform SDB. The method returns an array of strings, with each element holding a sentence.

This process is demonstrated in the following example. A try-with-resources block is used to open the en-sent.bin file, which contains a model. Then the paragraph string is processed. Next, various IO type exceptions are caught (if necessary). Finally, a for-each statement is used to display the sentences:

```
try (InputStream is = new FileInputStream(
        new File(getModelDir(), "en-sent.bin"))) {
    SentenceModel model = new SentenceModel(is);
    SentenceDetectorME detector = new SentenceDetectorME(model);
    String sentences[] = detector.sentDetect(paragraph);
    for (String sentence : sentences) {
        System.out.println(sentence);
    }
} catch (FileNotFoundException ex) {
    // Handle exception
} catch (IOException ex) {
    // Handle exception
}
```

On execution, we get the following output:

```
When determining the end of sentences we need to consider several
factors.
Sentences may end with exclamation marks!
Or possibly questions marks?
Within sentences we may find numbers like 3.14159, abbreviations such as
found in Mr. Smith, and possibly ellipses either within a sentence …, or
at the end of a sentence…
```

The output worked well for this paragraph. It caught both simple sentences and the more complex sentences. Of course, text that is processed is not always perfect. The following paragraph has extra spaces in some spots and is missing spaces where it needs them. This problem is likely to occur in the analysis of chat sessions:

```
paragraph = " This sentence starts with spaces and ends with "
    + "spaces . This sentence has no spaces between the next "
    + "one.This is the next one.";
```

When we use this paragraph with the previous example, we get the following output:

```
This sentence starts with spaces and ends with spaces  .
This sentence has no spaces between the next one.This is the next one.
```

The leading spaces of the first sentence were removed, but the ending spaces were not. The third sentence was not detected and was merged with the second sentence.

The `getSentenceProbabilities` method returns an array of doubles representing the confidence of the sentences detected from the last use of the `sentDetect` method. Add the following code after the for-each statement that displayed the sentences:

```
double probablities[] = detector.getSentenceProbabilities();
for (double probablity : probablities) {
    System.out.println(probablity);
}
```

By executing with the original paragraph, we get the following output:

```
0.9841708738988814
0.908052385070974
0.9130082376342675
1.0
```

The numbers reflects a high level of probabilities for the SDB effort.

Using the sentPosDetect method

The SentenceDetectorME class possesses a sentPosDetect method that returns Span objects for each sentence. Use the same code as found in the previous section, except for two changes: replace the sentDetect method with the sentPosDetect method, and the for-each statement with the method used here:

```
Span spans[] = sdetector.sentPosDetect(paragraph);
for (Span span : spans) {
    System.out.println(span);
}
```

The output that follows uses the original paragraph. The Span objects contain positional information returned from the default execution of the toString method:

```
[0..74)
[75..116)
[117..145)
[146..317)
```

The Span class possesses a number of methods. The next code sequence demonstrates the use of the getStart and getEnd methods to clearly show the text represented by those spans:

```
for (Span span : spans) {
    System.out.println(span + "[" + paragraph.substring(
        span.getStart(), span.getEnd()) +"]");
}
```

The output shows the sentences identified:

```
 [0..74)[When determining the end of sentences we need to consider
several factors.]
```

```
[75..116)[Sentences may end with exclamation marks!]
```

```
[117..145)[Or possibly questions marks?]
```

```
[146..317)[Within sentences we may find numbers like 3.14159,
abbreviations such as found in Mr. Smith, and possibly ellipses either
within a sentence …, or at the end of a sentence…]
```

There are a number of other Span methods that can be valuable. These are listed in the following table:

Method	Meaning
contains	An overloaded method that determines whether another Span object or index is contained with the target
crosses	Determines whether two spans overlap
length	The length of the span
startsWith	Determines whether the span starts the target span

Using the Stanford API

The Stanford NLP library supports several techniques used to perform sentence detection. In this section, we will demonstrate the process using the following classes:

- PTBTokenizer
- DocumentPreprocessor
- StanfordCoreNLP

Although all of them perform SBD, each uses a different approach to performing the process.

Using the PTBTokenizer class

The PTBTokenizer class uses rules to perform SBD and has a variety of tokenization options. The constructor for this class possesses three parameters:

- A Reader class that encapsulates the text to be processed
- An object that implements the LexedTokenFactory interface
- A string holding the tokenization options

These options allow us to specify the text, the tokenizer to be used, and any options that we may need to use for a specific text stream.

In the following code sequence, an instance of the StringReader class is created to encapsulate the text. The CoreLabelTokenFactory class is used with the options left as null for this example:

```
PTBTokenizer ptb = new PTBTokenizer(new StringReader(paragraph),
    new CoreLabelTokenFactory(), null);
```

We will use the `WordToSentenceProcessor` class to create a `List` instance of `List` class to hold the sentences and their tokens. Its `process` method takes the tokens produced by the `PTBTokenizer` instance to create the `List` of `list` class as shown here:

```
WordToSentenceProcessor wtsp = new WordToSentenceProcessor();
List<List<CoreLabel>> sents = wtsp.process(ptb.tokenize());
```

This `List` instance of `list` class can be displayed in several ways. In the next sequence, the `toString` method of the `List` class displays the list enclosed in brackets, with its elements separated by commas:

```
for (List<CoreLabel> sent : sents) {
    System.out.println(sent);
}
```

The output of this sequence produces the following:

```
[When, determining, the, end, of, sentences, we, need, to, consider,
several, factors, .]
```

```
[Sentences, may, end, with, exclamation, marks, !]
```

```
[Or, possibly, questions, marks, ?]
```

```
[Within, sentences, we, may, find, numbers, like, 3.14159, ,,
abbreviations, such, as, found, in, Mr., Smith, ,, and, possibly,
ellipses, either, within, a, sentence, ..., ,, or, at, the, end, of, a,
sentence, ...]
```

An alternate approach shown here displays each sentence on a separate line:

```
for (List<CoreLabel> sent : sents) {
    for (CoreLabel element : sent) {
        System.out.print(element + " ");
    }
    System.out.println();
}
```

The output is as follows:

```
When determining the end of sentences we need to consider several factors
.
```

```
Sentences may end with exclamation marks !
```

```
Or possibly questions marks ?
```

```
Within sentences we may find numbers like 3.14159 , abbreviations such as
found in Mr. Smith , and possibly ellipses either within a sentence ... ,
or at the end of a sentence ...
```

If we are only interested in the positions of the words and sentences, we can use the `endPosition` method, as illustrated here:

```
for (List<CoreLabel> sent : sents) {
    for (CoreLabel element : sent) {
        System.out.print(element.endPosition() + " ");
    }
    System.out.println();
}
```

When this is executed, we get the following output. The last number on each line is the index of the sentence boundary:

```
4 16 20 24 27 37 40 45 48 57 65 73 74
84 88 92 97 109 115 116
119 128 138 144 145
152 162 165 169 174 182 187 195 196 210 215 218 224 227 231 237 238 242
251 260 267 274 276 285 287 288 291 294 298 302 305 307 316 317
```

The first elements of each sentence are displayed in the following sequence along with its index:

```
for (List<CoreLabel> sent : sents) {
    System.out.println(sent.get(0) + " "
        + sent.get(0).beginPosition());
}
```

The output is as follows:

```
When 0
Sentences 75
Or 117
Within 146
```

If we are interested in the last elements of a sentence, we can use the following sequence. The number of elements of a list is used to display the terminating character and its ending position:

```
for (List<CoreLabel> sent : sents) {
    int size = sent.size();
    System.out.println(sent.get(size-1) + " "
        + sent.get(size-1).endPosition());
}
```

This will produce the following output:

```
.  74
!  116
?  145
... 317
```

There are a number of options available when the constructor of the `PTBTokenizer` class is invoked. These options are enclosed as the constructor's third parameter. The option string consists of the options separated by commas, as shown here:

```
"americanize=true,normalizeFractions=true,asciiQuotes=true".
```

Several of these options are listed in this table:

Option	Meaning
`invertible`	Used to indicate that the tokens and whitespace must be preserved so that the original string can be reconstructed
`tokenizeNLs`	Indicates that the ends of lines must be treated as tokens
`americanize`	If true, this will rewrite British spellings as American spellings
`normalizeAmpersandEntity`	Will convert the XML &amp character to an ampersand
`normalizeFractions`	Converts common fraction characters such as ½ to the long form (1/2)
`asciiQuotes`	Will convert quote characters to the simpler ' and " characters
`unicodeQuotes`	Will convert quote characters to characters that range from U+2018 to U+201D

The following sequence illustrates the use of this option string;

```
paragraph = "The colour of money is green. Common fraction "
    + "characters such as ½  are converted to the long form 1/2. "
    + "Quotes such as "cat" are converted to their simpler form.";
ptb = new PTBTokenizer(
    new StringReader(paragraph), new CoreLabelTokenFactory(),
    "americanize=true,normalizeFractions=true,asciiQuotes=true");
wtsp = new WordToSentenceProcessor();
```

```
sents = wtsp.process(ptb.tokenize());
for (List<CoreLabel> sent : sents) {
    for (CoreLabel element : sent) {
        System.out.print(element + " ");
    }
    System.out.println();
}
```

The output is as follows:

```
The color of money is green .
Common fraction characters such as 1/2 are converted to the long form 1/2
.
Quotes such as " cat " are converted to their simpler form .
```

The British spelling of the word "colour" was converted to its American equivalent. The fraction ½ was expanded to three characters: 1/2. In the last sentence, the smart quotes were converted to their simpler form.

Using the DocumentPreprocessor class

When an instance of the DocumentPreprocessor class is created, it uses its Reader parameter to produce a list of sentences. It also implements the Iterable interface, which makes it easy to traverse the list.

In the following example, the paragraph is used to create a StringReader object, and this object is used to instantiate the DocumentPreprocessor instance:

```
Reader reader = new StringReader(paragraph);
DocumentPreprocessor dp = new DocumentPreprocessor(reader);
for (List sentence : dp) {
    System.out.println(sentence);
}
```

On execution, we get the following output:

```
[When, determining, the, end, of, sentences, we, need, to, consider,
several, factors, .]
[Sentences, may, end, with, exclamation, marks, !]
[Or, possibly, questions, marks, ?]
[Within, sentences, we, may, find, numbers, like, 3.14159, ,,
abbreviations, such, as, found, in, Mr., Smith, ,, and, possibly,
ellipses, either, within, a, sentence, ..., ,, or, at, the, end, of, a,
sentence, ...]
```

By default, PTBTokenizer is used to tokenize the input. The setTokenizerFactory method can be used to specify a different tokenizer. There are several other methods that can be useful, as detailed in the following table:

Method	Purpose
setElementDelimiter	Its argument specifies an XML element. Only the text inside of those elements will be processed.
setSentenceDelimiter	The processor will assume that the string argument is a sentence delimiter.
setSentenceFinalPuncWords	Its string array argument specifies the end of sentences delimiters.
setKeepEmptySentences	When used with whitespace models, if its argument is true, then empty sentences will be retained.

The class can process either plain text or XML documents.

To demonstrate how an XML file can be processed, we will create a simple XML file called XMLText.xml, containing the following data:

```xml
<?xml version="1.0" encoding="UTF-8"?>
<?xml-stylesheet type="text/xsl"?>
<document>
    <sentences>
        <sentence id="1">
            <word>When</word>
            <word>the</word>
            <word>day</word>
            <word>is</word>
            <word>done</word>
            <word>we</word>
            <word>can</word>
            <word>sleep</word>
            <word>.</word>
        </sentence>
        <sentence id="2">
            <word>When</word>
            <word>the</word>
            <word>morning</word>
            <word>comes</word>
            <word>we</word>
            <word>can</word>
```

```
        <word>wake</word>
        <word>.</word>
    </sentence>
    <sentence id="3">
        <word>After</word>
        <word>that</word>
        <word>who</word>
        <word>knows</word>
        <word>.</word>
    </sentence>
</sentences>
</document>
```

We will reuse the code from the previous example. However, we will open the XMLText.xml file instead, and use DocumentPreprocessor.DocType.XML as the second argument of the constructor of the DocumentPreprocessor class, as shown next. This will specify that the processor should treat the text as XML text. In addition, we will specify that only those XML elements that are within the <sentence> tag should be processed:

```
try {
    Reader reader = new FileReader("XMLText.xml");
    DocumentPreprocessor dp = new DocumentPreprocessor(
        reader, DocumentPreprocessor.DocType.XML);
    dp.setElementDelimiter("sentence");
    for (List sentence : dp) {
        System.out.println(sentence);
    }
} catch (FileNotFoundException ex) {
    // Handle exception
}
```

The output of this example is as follows:

```
[When, the, day, is, done, we, can, sleep, .]
[When, the, morning, comes, we, can, wake, .]
[After, that, who, knows, .]
```

A cleaner output is possible using a ListIterator, as shown here:

```
for (List sentence : dp) {
    ListIterator list = sentence.listIterator();
     while (list.hasNext()) {
        System.out.print(list.next() + " ");
    }
    System.out.println();
}
```

Its output is the following:

```
When the day is done we can sleep .
When the morning comes we can wake .
After that who knows .
```

If we had not specified an element delimiter, then each word would have been displayed like this:

```
[When]
[the]
[day]
[is]
[done]
...
[who]
[knows]
[.]
```

Using the StanfordCoreNLP class

The StanfordCoreNLP class supports sentence detection using the ssplit annotator. In the following example, the tokenize and ssplit annotators are used. A pipeline object is created and the annotate method is applied against the pipeline using the paragraph as its argument:

```
Properties properties = new Properties();
properties.put("annotators", "tokenize, ssplit");
StanfordCoreNLP pipeline = new StanfordCoreNLP(properties);
Annotation annotation = new Annotation(paragraph);
pipeline.annotate(annotation);
```

The output contains a lot of information. Only the output for the first line is shown here:

```
Sentence #1 (13 tokens):
When determining the end of sentences we need to consider several
factors.
```

```
[Text=When CharacterOffsetBegin=0 CharacterOffsetEnd=4]
[Text=determining CharacterOffsetBegin=5 CharacterOffsetEnd=16]
[Text=the CharacterOffsetBegin=17 CharacterOffsetEnd=20]
[Text=end CharacterOffsetBegin=21 CharacterOffsetEnd=24] [Text=of
CharacterOffsetBegin=25 CharacterOffsetEnd=27] [Text=sentences
CharacterOffsetBegin=28 CharacterOffsetEnd=37] [Text=we
CharacterOffsetBegin=38 CharacterOffsetEnd=40] [Text=need
CharacterOffsetBegin=41 CharacterOffsetEnd=45] [Text=to
CharacterOffsetBegin=46 CharacterOffsetEnd=48] [Text=consider
CharacterOffsetBegin=49 CharacterOffsetEnd=57] [Text=several
CharacterOffsetBegin=58 CharacterOffsetEnd=65] [Text=factors
CharacterOffsetBegin=66 CharacterOffsetEnd=73] [Text=.
CharacterOffsetBegin=73 CharacterOffsetEnd=74]
```

Alternatively, we can use the `xmlPrint` method. This will produce the output in XML format, which can often be easier for extracting the information of interest. This method is shown here, and it requires that the `IOException` be handled:

```
try {
    pipeline.xmlPrint(annotation, System.out);
} catch (IOException ex) {
    // Handle exception
}
```

A partial listing of the output is as follows:

```
<?xml version="1.0" encoding="UTF-8"?>
<?xml-stylesheet href="CoreNLP-to-HTML.xsl" type="text/xsl"?>
<root>
  <document>
    <sentences>
      <sentence id="1">
        <tokens>
          <token id="1">
            <word>When</word>
            <CharacterOffsetBegin>0</CharacterOffsetBegin>
            <CharacterOffsetEnd>4</CharacterOffsetEnd>
          </token>
...
          <token id="34">
            <word>...</word>
            <CharacterOffsetBegin>316</CharacterOffsetBegin>
            <CharacterOffsetEnd>317</CharacterOffsetEnd>
          </token>
        </tokens>
      </sentence>
    </sentences>
  </document>
</root>
```

Using LingPipe

LingPipe uses a hierarchy of classes to support SBD, as shown in the following figure. At the base of this hierarchy is the `AbstractSentenceModel` class whose primary method is an overloaded `boundaryIndices` method. This method returns an integer array of a boundary index where each element of the array represents a sentence boundary.

Derived from this class is the `HeuristicSentenceModel` class. This class uses a series of Possible Stops, Impossible Penultimates, and Impossible Starts token sets. These were discussed earlier in the *Understanding SBD rules of LingPipe's HeuristicSentenceModel class* section of the chapter.

The `IndoEuropeanSentenceModel` and `MedlineSentenceModel` classes are derived from the `HeuristicSentenceModel` class. They have been trained for English and specialized medical text respectively. We will illustrate both of these classes.

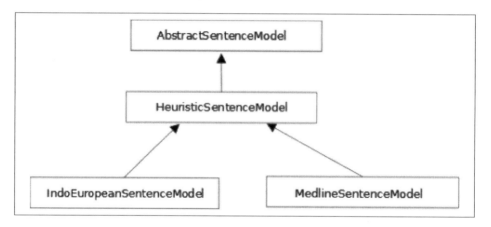

Using the IndoEuropeanSentenceModel class

The `IndoEuropeanSentenceModel` model is used for English text. Its two-argument constructor will specify:

- Whether the final token must be a stop
- Whether parentheses should be balanced

The default constructor does not force the final token to be a stop or expect that parentheses should be balanced. The sentence model needs to be used with a tokenizer. We will use the default constructor of the `IndoEuropeanTokenizerFactory` class for this purpose, as shown here:

```
TokenizerFactory TOKENIZER_FACTORY=
IndoEuropeanTokenizerFactory.INSTANCE;
SentenceModel sentenceModel = new IndoEuropeanSentenceModel();
```

A tokenizer is created and its `tokenize` method is invoked to populate two lists:

```
List<String> tokenList = new ArrayList<>();
List<String> whiteList = new ArrayList<>();
Tokenizer tokenizer= TOKENIZER_FACTORY.tokenizer(
    paragraph.toCharArray(),0, paragraph.length());
tokenizer.tokenize(tokenList, whiteList);
```

The `boundaryIndices` method returns an array of integer boundary indexes. The method requires two `String` array arguments containing tokens and whitespaces. The `tokenize` method used two `List` for these elements. This means we need to convert the `List` into equivalent arrays, as shown here:

```
String[] tokens = new String[tokenList.size()];
String[] whites = new String[whiteList.size()];
tokenList.toArray(tokens);
whiteList.toArray(whites);
```

We can then use the `boundaryIndices` method and display the indexes:

```
int[] sentenceBoundaries=
sentenceModel.boundaryIndices(tokens, whites);
for(int boundary : sentenceBoundaries) {
    System.out.println(boundary);
}
```

The output is shown here:

12

19

24

To display the actual sentences, we will use the following sequence. The whitespace indexes are one off from the token:

```
int start = 0;
for(int boundary : sentenceBoundaries) {
    while(start<=boundary) {
```

```
        System.out.print(tokenList.get(start)
    + whiteList.get(start+1));
        start++;
    }
    System.out.println();
}
```

The following output is the result:

When determining the end of sentences we need to consider several factors.

Sentences may end with exclamation marks!

Or possibly questions marks?

Unfortunately, it missed the last sentence. This is due to the last sentence ending in an ellipsis. If we add a period to the end of the sentence, we get the following output:

When determining the end of sentences we need to consider several factors.

Sentences may end with exclamation marks!

Or possibly questions marks?

Within sentences we may find numbers like 3.14159, abbreviations such as found in Mr. Smith, and possibly ellipses either within a sentence …, or at the end of a sentence….

Using the SentenceChunker class

An alternative approach is to use the SentenceChunker class to perform SBD. The constructor of this class requires a TokenizerFactory object and a SentenceModel object, as shown here:

```
TokenizerFactory tokenizerfactory =
IndoEuropeanTokenizerFactory.INSTANCE;
SentenceModel sentenceModel = new IndoEuropeanSentenceModel();
```

The SentenceChunker instance is created using the tokenizer factory and sentence instances:

```
SentenceChunker sentenceChunker =
    new SentenceChunker(tokenizerfactory, sentenceModel);
```

The SentenceChunker class implements the Chunker interface that uses a chunk method. This method returns an object that implements the Chunking interface. This object specifies "chunks" of text with a character sequence (CharSequence).

The chunk method uses a character array and indexes within the array to specify which portions of the text need to be processed. A Chunking object is returned like this:

```
Chunking chunking = sentenceChunker.chunk(
    paragraph.toCharArray(),0, paragraph.length());
```

We will use the Chunking object for two purposes. First, we will use its chunkSet method to return a Set of Chunk objects. Then we will obtain a string holding all the sentences:

```
Set<Chunk> sentences = chunking.chunkSet();
String slice = chunking.charSequence().toString();
```

A Chunk object stores character offsets of the sentence boundaries. We will use its start and end methods in conjunction with the slice to display the sentences, as shown next. Each element, sentence, holds the sentence's boundary. We use this information to display each sentence in the slice:

```
for (Chunk sentence : sentences) {
    System.out.println("[" + slice.substring(sentence.start(),
        sentence.end()) + "]");
}
```

The following is the output. However, it still has problems with sentences ending with an ellipsis, so a period has been added to the end of the last sentence before the text is processed.

```
[When determining the end of sentences we need to consider several
factors.]

[Sentences may end with exclamation marks!]

[Or possibly questions marks?]

[Within sentences we may find numbers like 3.14159, abbreviations such as
found in Mr. Smith, and possibly ellipses either within a sentence …, or
at the end of a sentence….]
```

Although the IndoEuropeanSentenceModel class works reasonably well for English text, it may not always work well for specialized text. In the next section, we will examine the use of the MedlineSentenceModel class, which has been trained to work with medical text.

Using the MedlineSentenceModel class

The LingPipe sentence model uses **MEDLINE**, which is a large collection of biomedical literature. This collection is stored in XML format and is maintained by the United States National Library of Medicine (http://www.nlm.nih.gov/).

LingPipe uses its MedlineSentenceModel class to perform SBD. This model has been trained against the MEDLINE data. It uses simple text and tokenizes it into tokens and whitespace. The MEDLINE model is then used to find the text's sentences.

In the next example, we will use a paragraph from http://www.ncbi.nlm.nih.gov/pmc/articles/PMC3139422/ to demonstrate the use of the model, as declared here:

```
paragraph = "HepG2 cells were obtained from the American Type
Culture "
        + "Collection (Rockville, MD, USA) and were used only until "
        + "passage 30. They were routinely grown at 37°C in Dulbecco's "
        + "modified Eagle's medium (DMEM) containing 10 % fetal bovine "
        + "serum (FBS), 2 mM glutamine, 1 mM sodium pyruvate, and 25 "
        + "mM glucose (Invitrogen, Carlsbad, CA, USA) in a humidified "
        + "atmosphere containing 5% CO2. For precursor and 13C-sugar "
        + "experiments, tissue culture treated polystyrene 35 mm "
        + "dishes (Corning Inc, Lowell, MA, USA) were seeded with 2 "
        + "x 106 cells and grown to confluency in DMEM.";
```

The code that follows is based on the SentenceChunker class, as demonstrated in the previous section. The difference is in the use of the MedlineSentenceModel class:

```
TokenizerFactory tokenizerfactory =
    IndoEuropeanTokenizerFactory.INSTANCE;
MedlineSentenceModel sentenceModel = new
    MedlineSentenceModel();
SentenceChunker sentenceChunker =
    new SentenceChunker(tokenizerfactory,
sentenceModel);
Chunking chunking = sentenceChunker.chunk(
    paragraph.toCharArray(), 0, paragraph.length());
Set<Chunk> sentences = chunking.chunkSet();
String slice = chunking.charSequence().toString();
for (Chunk sentence : sentences) {
    System.out.println("["
        + slice.substring(sentence.start(),
sentence.end())
        + "]");
}
```

The output is as follows:

```
[HepG2 cells were obtained from the American Type Culture Collection
(Rockville, MD, USA) and were used only until passage 30.]

[They were routinely grown at 37°C in Dulbecco's modified Eagle's medium
(DMEM) containing 10 % fetal bovine serum (FBS), 2 mM glutamine, 1 mM
sodium pyruvate, and 25 mM glucose (Invitrogen, Carlsbad, CA, USA) in a
humidified atmosphere containing 5% CO2.]

[For precursor and 13C-sugar experiments, tissue culture treated
polystyrene 35 mm dishes (Corning Inc, Lowell, MA, USA) were seeded with
2 x 106 cells and grown to confluency in DMEM.]
```

When executed against medical text, this model will perform better than other models.

Training a Sentence Detector model

We will use OpenNLP's `SentenceDetectorME` class to illustrate the training process. This class has a static `train` method that uses sample sentences found in a file. The method returns a model that is usually serialized to a file for later use.

Models use specially annotated data to clearly specify where a sentence ends. Frequently, a large file is used to provide a good sample for training purposes. Part of the file is used for training purposes, and the rest is used to verify the model after it has been trained.

The training file used by OpenNLP consists of one sentence per line. Usually, at least 10 to 20 sample sentences are needed to avoid processing errors. To demonstrate the process, we will use a file called `sentence.train`. It consists of *Chapter 5, Twenty Thousand Leagues under the Sea by Jules Verne*. The text of the book can be found at `http://www.gutenberg.org/files/164/164-h/164-h.htm#chap05`. The file can be downloaded from `www.packtpub.com`.

A `FileReader` object is used to open the file. This object is used as the argument of the `PlainTextByLineStream` constructor. The stream that results consists of a string for each line of the file. This is used as the argument of the `SentenceSampleStream` constructor, which converts the sentence strings to `SentenceSample` objects. These objects hold the beginning index of each sentence. This process is shown next, where the statements are enclosed in a try block to handle exceptions that may be thrown by these statements:

```
try {
    ObjectStream<String> lineStream = new PlainTextByLineStream(
        new FileReader("sentence.train"));
```

```
ObjectStream<SentenceSample> sampleStream
    = new SentenceSampleStream(lineStream);
...
} catch (FileNotFoundException ex) {
    // Handle exception
} catch (IOException ex) {
    // Handle exception
}
```

Now the `train` method can be used like this:

```
SentenceModel model = SentenceDetectorME.train("en",
    sampleStream, true,
    null, TrainingParameters.defaultParams());
```

The output of the method is a trained model. The parameters of this method are detailed in the following table:

Parameter	Meaning
`"en"`	Specifies that the language of the text is English
`sampleStream`	The training text stream
`true`	Specifies whether end tokens shown should be used
`null`	A dictionary for abbreviations
`TrainingParameters.defaultParams()`	Specifies that the default training parameters should be used

In the following sequence, an `OutputStream` is created and used to save the model in the `modelFile` file. This allows the model to be reused for other applications:

```
OutputStream modelStream = new BufferedOutputStream(
    new FileOutputStream("modelFile"));
model.serialize(modelStream);
```

The output of this process is as follows. All the iterations have not been shown here to save space. The default cuts off indexing events to 5 and iterations to 100:

```
Indexing events using cutoff of 5

    Computing event counts...  done. 93 events
    Indexing...  done.
Sorting and merging events... done. Reduced 93 events to 63.
```

```
Done indexing.
Incorporating indexed data for training...
done.
      Number of Event Tokens: 63
         Number of Outcomes: 2
      Number of Predicates: 21
...done.
Computing model parameters ...
Performing 100 iterations.
  1:  ... loglikelihood=-64.4626877920749       0.9032258064516129
  2:  ... loglikelihood=-31.11084296202819      0.9032258064516129
  3:  ... loglikelihood=-26.418795734248626     0.9032258064516129
  4:  ... loglikelihood=-24.327956749903198     0.9032258064516129
  5:  ... loglikelihood=-22.766489585258565     0.9032258064516129
  6:  ... loglikelihood=-21.46379347841989      0.9139784946236559
  7:  ... loglikelihood=-20.356036369911394     0.9139784946236559
  8:  ... loglikelihood=-19.406935608514992     0.9139784946236559
  9:  ... loglikelihood=-18.58725539754483      0.9139784946236559
 10:  ... loglikelihood=-17.873030559849326     0.9139784946236559
...
 99:  ... loglikelihood=-7.214933901940582      0.978494623655914
100:  ... loglikelihood=-7.183774954664058      0.978494623655914
```

Using the Trained model

We can then use the model as illustrated in the next code sequence. This is based on the techniques illustrated in *Using the SentenceDetectorME class* earlier in this chapter:

```java
try (InputStream is = new FileInputStream(
        new File(getModelDir(), "modelFile"))) {
    SentenceModel model = new SentenceModel(is);
    SentenceDetectorME detector = new
    SentenceDetectorME(model);
    String sentences[] = detector.sentDetect(paragraph);
    for (String sentence : sentences) {
        System.out.println(sentence);
    }
} catch (FileNotFoundException ex) {
    // Handle exception
```

```
} catch (IOException ex) {
   // Handle exception
}
```

The output is as follows:

When determining the end of sentences we need to consider several factors.

Sentences may end with exclamation marks! Or possibly questions marks?

Within sentences we may find numbers like 3.14159,

abbreviations such as found in Mr.

Smith, and possibly ellipses either within a sentence …, or at the end of a sentence…

This model did not process the last sentence very well, which reflects a mismatch between the sample text and the text the model is used against. Using relevant training data is important. Otherwise, downstream tasks based on this output will suffer.

Evaluating the model using the SentenceDetectorEvaluator class

We reserved a part of the sample file for evaluation purposes so that we can use the SentenceDetectorEvaluator class to evaluate the model. We modified the sentence.train file by extracting the last ten sentences and placing them in a file called evalSample. Then we used this file to evaluate the model. In the next example, we've reused the lineStream and sampleStream variables to create a stream of SentenceSample objects based on the file's contents:

```
lineStream = new PlainTextByLineStream(
    new FileReader("evalSample"));
sampleStream = new SentenceSampleStream(lineStream);
```

An instance of the SentenceDetectorEvaluator class is created using the previously created SentenceDetectorME class variable detector. The second argument of the constructor is a SentenceDetectorEvaluationMonitor object, which we will not use here. Then the evaluate method is called:

```
SentenceDetectorEvaluator sentenceDetectorEvaluator
    = new SentenceDetectorEvaluator(detector, null);
sentenceDetectorEvaluator.evaluate(sampleStream);
```

The `getFMeasure` method will return an instance of the `FMeasure` class that provides measurements of the quality of the model:

```
System.out.println(sentenceDetectorEvaluator.getFMeasure());
```

The output follows. Precision is the fraction of correct instances that are included, and recall reflects the sensitivity of the model. F-measure is a score that combines recall and precision. In essence, it reflects how well the model works. It is best to keep the precision above 90 percent for tokenization and SBD tasks:

```
Precision: 0.8181818181818182

Recall: 0.9

F-Measure: 0.8571428571428572
```

Summary

We discussed many of the issues that make sentence detection a difficult task. These include problems that result from periods being used for numbers and abbreviations. The use of ellipses and embedded quotes can also be problematic.

Java does provide a couple of techniques to detect the end of a sentence. We saw how regular expressions and the `BreakIterator` class can be used. These techniques are useful for simple sentences, but they do not work that well for more complicated sentences.

The use of various NLP APIs was also illustrated. Some of these process the text based on rules, while others use models. We also demonstrated how models can be trained and evaluated.

In the next chapter, you will learn how to find people and things with text.

4

Finding People and Things

The process of finding people and things is referred to as **Named Entity Recognition (NER)**. Entities such as people and places are associated with categories that have names, which identify what they are. A named category can be as simple as "people". Common entity types include:

- People
- Locations
- Organizations
- Money
- Time
- URLs

Finding names, locations, and various things in a document are important and useful NLP tasks. They are used in many places such as conducting simple searches, processing queries, resolving references, the disambiguation of text, and finding the meaning of text. For example, NER is sometimes interested in only finding those entities that belong to a single category. Using categories, the search can be isolated to those item types. Other NLP tasks use NER such as in POS taggers and in performing cross-referencing tasks.

The NER process involves two tasks:

- Detection of entities
- Classification of entities

Detection is concerned with finding the position of an entity within text. Once it is are located, it is important to determine what type of entity was discovered. After these two tasks have been performed, the results can be used to solve other tasks such as searching and determining the meaning of the text. For example, identifying names from a movie or book review and helping to find other movies or books that might be of interest. Extracting location information can assist in providing references to nearby services.

Why NER is difficult?

Like many NLP tasks, NER is not always simple. Although the tokenization of a text will reveal its components, understanding what they are can be difficult. Using proper nouns will not always work because of the ambiguity of language. For example, Penny and Faith, while valid names, they may also be used for a measurement of currency and a belief, respectively. We can also find words such as Georgia are used as a name of a country, a state, and a person.

Some phrases can be challenging. The phrase "Metropolitan Convention and Exhibit Hall" may contain words that in themselves are valid entities. When the domain is well known, a list of entities can be very useful and easy to implement.

NER is typically applied at the sentence level, otherwise a phrase can easily span a sentence leading to incorrect identification of an entity. For example, in the following sentence:

"Bob went south. Dakota went west."

If we ignored the sentence boundaries, then we could inadvertently find the location entity South Dakota.

Specialized text such as URLs, e-mail addresses, and specialized numbers can be difficult to isolate. This identification is made even more difficult if we have to take into account variations of the entity form. For example, are parentheses used with phone numbers? Are dashes, or periods, or some other character used to separate its parts? Do we need to consider international phone numbers?

These factors contribute to the need for good NER techniques.

Techniques for name recognition

There are a number of NER techniques available. Some use regular expressions and others are based on a predefined dictionary. Regular expressions have a lot of expressive power and can isolate entities. A dictionary of entity names can be compared to tokens of text to find matches.

Another common NER approach uses trained models to detect their presence. These models are dependent on the type of entity we are looking for and the target language. A model that works well for one domain, such as web pages, may not work well for a different domain, such as medical journals.

When a model is trained, it uses an annotated block of text, which identifies the entities of interest. To measure how well a model has been trained, several measures are used:

- **Precision**: It is the percentage of entities found that match exactly the spans found in the evaluation data
- **Recall**: It is the percentage of entities defined in the corpus that were found in the same location
- **Performance measure**: It is the harmonic mean of precision and recall given by $F1 = 2 * Precision * Recall / (Recall + Precision)$

We will use these measures when we cover the evaluation of models.

NER is also known as entity identification and entity chunking. **Chunking** is the analysis of text to identify its parts such as nouns, verbs, or other components. As humans, we tend to chunk a sentence into distinct parts. These parts form a structure that we use to determine its meaning. The NER process will create spans of text such as "Queen of England". However, there may be other entities within these spans such as "England".

Lists and regular expressions

One technique is to use lists of "standard" entities along with regular expressions to identify the named entities. Named entities are sometimes referred to as proper nouns. The standard entities list could be a list of states, common names, months, or frequently referenced locations. Gazetteers, which are lists that contain geographical information used with maps, provide a source of location-related entities. However, maintaining such lists can be time consuming. They can also be specific to language and locale. Making changes to the list can be tedious. We will demonstrate this approach in the *Using the ExactDictionaryChunker class* section later in this chapter.

Regular expressions can be useful in identifying entities. Their powerful syntax provides enough flexibility in many situations to accurately isolate the entity of interest. However, this flexibility can also make it difficult to understand and maintain. We will demonstrate several regular expression approaches in this chapter.

Statistical classifiers

Statistical classifiers determine whether a word is a start of an entity, the continuation of an entity, or not an entity at all. Sample text is tagged to isolate entities. Once a classifier has been developed, it can be trained on different sets of data for different problem domains. The disadvantage of this approach is that it requires someone to annotate the sample text, which is a time-consuming process. In addition, it is domain dependent.

We will examine several approaches to perform NER. First, we will start by explaining how regular expressions are used to identify entities.

Using regular expressions for NER

Regular expressions can be used to identify entities in a document. We will investigate two general approaches:

- The first one uses regular expressions as supported by Java. These can be useful in situations where the entities are relatively simple and consistent in their form.

- The second approach uses classes designed to specifically use regular expressions. To demonstrate this, we will use LingPipe's RegExChunker class.

When working with regular expressions, it is advantageous to avoid reinventing the wheel. There are many sources for predefined and tested expressions. One such library can be found at http://regexlib.com/Default.aspx. We will use several of the regular expressions in this library for our examples.

To test how well these approaches work, we will use the following text for most of our examples:

```
private static String regularExpressionText
    = "He left his email address (rgb@colorworks.com) and his "
    + "phone number,800-555-1234. We believe his current address "
    + "is 100 Washington Place, Seattle, CO 12345-1234. I "
    + "understand you can also call at 123-555-1234 between "
    + "8:00 AM and 4:30 most days. His URL is http://example.com "
    + "and he was born on February 25, 1954 or 2/25/1954.";
```

Using Java's regular expressions to find entities

To demonstrate how these expressions can be used, we will start with several simple examples. The initial example starts with the following declaration. It is a simple expression designed to identify certain types of phone numbers:

```
String phoneNumberRE = "\\d{3}-\\d{3}-\\d{4}";
```

We will use the following code to test our simple expressions. The `Pattern` class' `compile` method takes a regular expression and compiles it into a `Pattern` object. Its `matcher` method can then be executed against the target text, which returns a `Matcher` object. This object allows us to repeatedly identify regular expression matches:

```
Pattern pattern = Pattern.compile(phoneNumberRE);
Matcher matcher = pattern.matcher(regularExpressionText);
while (matcher.find()) {
    System.out.println(matcher.group() + " [" + matcher.start()
        + ":" + matcher.end() + "]");
}
```

The `find` method will return `true` when a match occurs. Its `group` method returns the text that matches the expression. Its `start` and `end` methods give us the position of the matched text in the target text.

When executed, we will get the following output:

```
800-555-1234 [68:80]
123-555-1234 [196:208]
```

A number of other regular expressions can be used in a similar manner. These are listed in the following table. The third column is the output produced when the corresponding regular expression is used in the previous code sequence:

Entity type	Regular expression	Output
URL	`\\b(https?|ftp|file|ldap)://[-A-Za-z0-9+&@#/%?=~_|!:,.;]*[-A-Za-z0-9+&@#/%=~_|]`	`http://example.com [256:274]`
ZIP code	`[0-9]{5}(\\-?[0-9]{4})?`	`12345-1234 [150:160]`
E-mail	`[a-zA-Z0-9'._%+-]+@(?:[a-zA-Z0-9-]+\\.)+[a-zA-Z]{2,4}`	`rgb@colorworks.com [27:45]`

Entity type	Regular expression	Output
Time	`((([0-1]?[0-9])|([2][0-3])):([0-5]?[0-9])(:([0-5]?[0-9]))?`	8:00 [217:221] 4:30 [229:233]
Date	`((0?[13578]|10|12)(-|\\/)(([1-9])|(0[1-9])|([12])([0-9]?)|(3[01]?))(-|\\/)((19)([2-9])(\\d{1})|(20)([01])(\\d{1})|([8901])(\\d{1}))|(0?[2469]|11)(-|\\/)(([1-9])|(0[1-9])|([12])([0-9]?)|(3[0]?))(-|\\/)((19)([2-9])(\\d{1})|(20)([01])(\\d{1})|([8901])(\\d{1})))`	2/25/1954 [315:324]

There are many other regular expressions that we could have used. However, these examples illustrate the basic technique. As demonstrated with the date regular expression, some of these can be quite complex.

It is common for regular expressions to miss some entities and to falsely report other non-entities as entities. For example, if we replace the text with the following expression:

```
regularExpressionText =
    "(888)555-1111 888-SEL-HIGH 888-555-2222-J88-W3S";
```

Executing the code will return this:

888-555-2222 [27:39]

It missed the first two phone numbers and falsely reported the "part number" as a phone number.

We can also search for more than one regular expression at a time using the | operator. In the following statement, three regular expressions are combined using this operator. They are declared using the corresponding entries in the previous table:

```
Pattern pattern = Pattern.compile(phoneNumberRE + "|"
    + timeRE + "|" + emailRegEx);
```

When executed using the original `regularExpressionText` text defined at the beginning of the previous section, we get the following output:

```
rgb@colorworks.com [27:45]

800-555-1234 [68:80]

123-555-1234 [196:208]

8:00 [217:221]

4:30 [229:233]
```

Using LingPipe's RegExChunker class

The `RegExChunker` class uses chunks to find entities in text. The class uses a regular expression to represent an entity. Its `chunk` method returns a `Chunking` object that can be used as we did in our earlier examples.

The `RegExChunker` class' constructor takes three arguments:

- `String`: This is a regular expression
- `String`: This is a type of entity or category
- `double`: A value for score

We will demonstrate this class using a regular expression representing time as shown in the next example. The regular expression is the same as used in *Using Java's regular expressions to find entities* earlier in this chapter. The `Chunker` instance is then created:

```
String timeRE =
    "(([0-1]?[0-9])|([2][0-3])):([0-5]?[0-9])(:([0-5]?[0-9]))?";
        Chunker chunker = new RegExChunker(timeRE,"time",1.0);
```

The `chunk` method is used along with the `displayChunkSet` method, as shown here:

```
Chunking chunking = chunker.chunk(regularExpressionText);
Set<Chunk> chunkSet = chunking.chunkSet();
displayChunkSet(chunker, regularExpressionText);
```

The `displayChunkSet` method is shown in the following code segment. The `chunkSet` method returns a `Set` collection of `Chunk` instances. We can use various methods to display specific parts of the chunk:

```
public void displayChunkSet(Chunker chunker, String text) {
    Chunking chunking = chunker.chunk(text);
    Set<Chunk> set = chunking.chunkSet();
    for (Chunk chunk : set) {
```

```
        System.out.println("Type: " + chunk.type() + " Entity: ["
            + text.substring(chunk.start(), chunk.end())
            + "] Score: " + chunk.score());
    }
}
```

The output is as follows:

Type: time Entity: [8:00] Score: 1.0

Type: time Entity: [4:30] Score: 1.0+95

Alternately, we can declare a simple class to encapsulate the regular expression, which lends itself for reuse in other situations. Next, the `TimeRegexChunker` class is declared and it supports the identification of time entities:

```
public class TimeRegexChunker extends RegExChunker {
    private final static String TIME_RE =
        "(([0-1]?[0-9])|([2][0-3])):([0-5]?[0-9])(:([0-5]?[0-9]))?";
    private final static String CHUNK_TYPE = "time";
    private final static double CHUNK_SCORE = 1.0;

    public TimeRegexChunker() {
        super(TIME_RE,CHUNK_TYPE,CHUNK_SCORE);
    }
}
```

To use this class, replace this section's initial declaration of `chunker` with the following declaration:

```
Chunker chunker = new TimeRegexChunker();
```

The output will be the same as before.

Using NLP APIs

We will demonstrate the NER process using OpenNLP, Stanford API, and LingPipe. Each of these provide alternate techniques that can often do a good job of identifying entities in the text. The following declaration will serve as the sample text to demonstrate the APIs:

```
String sentences[] = {"Joe was the last person to see Fred. ",
    "He saw him in Boston at McKenzie's pub at 3:00 where he "
    + " paid $2.45 for an ale. ",
    "Joe wanted to go to Vermont for the day to visit a cousin who "
    + "works at IBM, but Sally and he had to look for Fred"};
```

Using OpenNLP for NER

We will demonstrate the use of the TokenNameFinderModel class to perform NLP using the OpenNLP API. Additionally, we will demonstrate how to determine the probability that the entity identified is correct.

The general approach is to convert the text into a series of tokenized sentences, create an instance of the TokenNameFinderModel class using an appropriate model, and then use the find method to identify the entities in the text.

The following example demonstrates the use of the TokenNameFinderModel class. We will use a simple sentence initially and then use multiple sentences. The sentence is defined here:

```
String sentence = "He was the last person to see Fred.";
```

We will use the models found in the en-token.bin and en-ner-person.bin files for the tokenizer and name finder models, respectively. The InputStream object for these files is opened using a try-with-resources block, as shown here:

```
try (InputStream tokenStream = new FileInputStream(
        new File(getModelDir(), "en-token.bin"));
        InputStream modelStream = new FileInputStream(
            new File(getModelDir(), "en-ner-person.bin"));) {

    ...


} catch (Exception ex) {
    // Handle exceptions
}
```

Within the try block, the TokenizerModel and Tokenizer objects are created:

```
TokenizerModel tokenModel = new TokenizerModel(tokenStream);
Tokenizer tokenizer = new TokenizerME(tokenModel);
```

Next, an instance of the NameFinderME class is created using the person model:

```
TokenNameFinderModel entityModel =
    new TokenNameFinderModel(modelStream);
NameFinderME nameFinder = new NameFinderME(entityModel);
```

We can now use the tokenize method to tokenize the text and the find method to identify the person in the text. The find method will use the tokenized String array as input and return an array of Span objects, as shown:

```
String tokens[] = tokenizer.tokenize(sentence);
Span nameSpans[] = nameFinder.find(tokens);
```

We discussed the span class in *Chapter 3, Finding Sentences*. As you may remember, this class holds positional information about the entities found. The actual string entities are still in the tokens array:

The following for statement displays the person found in the sentence. Its positional information and the person are displayed on separate lines:

```
for (int i = 0; i < nameSpans.length; i++) {
    System.out.println("Span: " + nameSpans[i].toString());
    System.out.println("Entity: "
        + tokens[nameSpans[i].getStart()]);
}
```

The output is as follows:

Span: [7..9) person

Entity: Fred

We will often work with multiple sentences. To demonstrate this, we will use the previously defined sentences string array. The previous for statement is replaced with the following sequence. The tokenize method is invoked against each sentence and then the entity information is displayed as earlier:

```
for (String sentence : sentences) {
    String tokens[] = tokenizer.tokenize(sentence);
    Span nameSpans[] = nameFinder.find(tokens);
    for (int i = 0; i < nameSpans.length; i++) {
        System.out.println("Span: " + nameSpans[i].toString());
        System.out.println("Entity: "
            + tokens[nameSpans[i].getStart()]);
    }
    System.out.println();
}
```

The output is as follows. There is an extra blank line between the two people detected because the second sentence did not contain a person:

Span: [0..1) person

Entity: Joe

Span: [7..9) person

Entity: Fred

Span: [0..1) person

```
Entity: Joe
Span: [19..20) person
Entity: Sally
Span: [26..27) person
Entity: Fred
```

Determining the accuracy of the entity

When the `TokenNameFinderModel` identifies entities in text, it computes a probability for that entity. We can access this information using the `probs` method as shown in the following line of code. This method returns an array of doubles, which corresponds to the elements of the `nameSpans` array:

```
double[] spanProbs = nameFinder.probs(nameSpans);
```

Add this statement to the previous example immediately after the use of the `find` method. Then add the next statement at the end of the nested for statement:

```
System.out.println("Probability: " + spanProbs[i]);
```

When the example is executed, you will get the following output. The probability fields reflect the confidence level of the entity assignment. For the first entity, the model is 80.529 percent confident that "Joe" is a person:

```
Span: [0..1) person
Entity: Joe
Probability: 0.8052914774025202
Span: [7..9) person
Entity: Fred
Probability: 0.9042160889302772

Span: [0..1) person
Entity: Joe
Probability: 0.9620970782763985
Span: [19..20) person
Entity: Sally
Probability: 0.964568603518126
Span: [26..27) person
Entity: Fred
Probability: 0.990383039618594
```

Using other entity types

OpenNLP supports different libraries as listed in the following table. These models can be downloaded from `http://opennlp.sourceforge.net/models-1.5/`. The prefix, `en`, specifies English as the language and `ner` indicates that the model is for NER.

English finder models	Filename
Location name finder model	`en-ner-location.bin`
Money name finder model	`en-ner-money.bin`
Organization name finder model	`en-ner-organization.bin`
Percentage name finder model	`en-ner-percentage.bin`
Person name finder model	`en-ner-person.bin`
Time name finder model	`en-ner-time.bin`

If we modify the statement to use a different model file, we can see how they work against the sample sentences:

```
InputStream modelStream = new FileInputStream(
    new File(getModelDir(), "en-ner-time.bin"));) {
```

 When the `en-ner-money.bin` model is used, the index in the tokens array in the earlier code sequence has to be increased by one. Otherwise, all that is returned is the dollar sign.

The various outputs are shown in the following table.

Model	Output
`en-ner-location.bin`	Span: [4..5) location Entity: Boston Probability: 0.8656908776583051 Span: [5..6) location Entity: Vermont Probability: 0.9732488014011262
`en-ner-money.bin`	Span: [14..16) money Entity: 2.45 Probability: 0.7200919701507937

Model	Output
en-ner-organization. bin	Span: [16..17) organization
	Entity: IBM
	Probability: 0.9256970736336729
en-ner-time.bin	The model was not able to detect time in this text sequence

The model failed to find the time entities in the sample text. This illustrates that the model did not have enough confidence that it found any time entities in the text.

Processing multiple entity types

We can also handle multiple entity types at the same time. This involves creating instances of the `NameFinderME` class based on each model within a loop and applying the model against each sentence, keeping track of the entities as they are found.

We will illustrate this process with the following example. It requires rewriting the previous try block to create the `InputStream` instance within the block, as shown here:

```
try {
    InputStream tokenStream = new FileInputStream(
        new File(getModelDir(), "en-token.bin"));
    TokenizerModel tokenModel = new TokenizerModel(tokenStream);
    Tokenizer tokenizer = new TokenizerME(tokenModel);
    ...
} catch (Exception ex) {
    // Handle exceptions
}
```

Within the try block, we will define a `string` array to hold the names of the model files. As shown here, we will use models for people, locations, and organizations:

```
String modelNames[] = {"en-ner-person.bin",
    "en-ner-location.bin", "en-ner-organization.bin"};
```

An `ArrayList` instance is created to hold the entities as they are discovered:

```
ArrayList<String> list = new ArrayList();
```

A for-each statement is used to load one model at a time and then to create an instance of the NameFinderME class:

```
for(String name : modelNames) {
    TokenNameFinderModel entityModel = new TokenNameFinderModel(
        new FileInputStream(new File(getModelDir(), name)));
    NameFinderME nameFinder = new NameFinderME(entityModel);
    ...
}
```

Previously, we did not try to identify which sentences the entities were found in. This is not hard to do but we need to use a simple for statement instead of a for-each statement to keep track of the sentence indexes. This is shown in the following example, where the previous example has been modified to use the integer variable index to keep the sentences. Otherwise, the code works the same way as earlier:

```
for (int index = 0; index < sentences.length; index++) {
    String tokens[] = tokenizer.tokenize(sentences[index]);
    Span nameSpans[] = nameFinder.find(tokens);
    for(Span span : nameSpans) {
        list.add("Sentence: " + index
            + " Span: " + span.toString() + " Entity: "
            + tokens[span.getStart()]);
    }
}
```

The entities discovered are then displayed:

```
for(String element : list) {
    System.out.println(element);
}
```

The output is as follows:

```
Sentence: 0 Span: [0..1) person Entity: Joe
Sentence: 0 Span: [7..9) person Entity: Fred
Sentence: 2 Span: [0..1) person Entity: Joe
Sentence: 2 Span: [19..20) person Entity: Sally
Sentence: 2 Span: [26..27) person Entity: Fred
Sentence: 1 Span: [4..5) location Entity: Boston
Sentence: 2 Span: [5..6) location Entity: Vermont
Sentence: 2 Span: [16..17) organization Entity: IBM
```

Using the Stanford API for NER

We will demonstrate the CRFClassifier class as used to perform NER. This class implements what is known as a linear chain **Conditional Random Field (CRF)** sequence model.

To demonstrate the use of the CRFClassifier class, we will start with a declaration of the classifier file string, as shown here:

```
String model = getModelDir() +
    "\\english.conll.4class.distsim.crf.ser.gz";
```

The classifier is then created using the model:

```
CRFClassifier<CoreLabel> classifier =
    CRFClassifier.getClassifierNoExceptions(model);
```

The classify method takes a single string representing the text to be processed. To use the sentences text, we need to convert it to a simple string:

```
String sentence = "";
for (String element : sentences) {
    sentence += element;
}
```

The classify method is then applied to the text.

```
List<List<CoreLabel>> entityList = classifier.classify(sentence);
```

A List instance of List instances of CoreLabel objects is returned. The object returned is a list that contains another list. The contained list is a List instance of CoreLabel objects. The CoreLabel class represents a word with additional information attached to it. The "internal" list contains a list of these words. In the outer for-each statement in the following code sequence, the reference variable, internalList, represents one sentence of the text. In the inner for-each statement, each word in that inner list is displayed. The word method returns the word and the get method returns the type of the word.

The words and their types are then displayed:

```
for (List<CoreLabel> internalList: entityList) {
    for (CoreLabel coreLabel : internalList) {
        String word = coreLabel.word();
        String category = coreLabel.get(
            CoreAnnotations.AnswerAnnotation.class);
        System.out.println(word + ":" + category);
    }
}
```

Part of the output follows. It has been truncated because every word is displayed. The o represents the "Other" category:

```
Joe:PERSON

was:O

the:O

last:O

person:O

to:O

see:O

Fred:PERSON

.:O

He:O

...

look:O

for:O

Fred:PERSON
```

To filter out the words that are not relevant, replace the `println` statement with the following statements. This will eliminate the other categories:

```java
if (!"O".equals(category)) {
    System.out.println(word + ":" + category);
}
```

The output is simpler now:

```
Joe:PERSON

Fred:PERSON

Boston:LOCATION

McKenzie:PERSON

Joe:PERSON

Vermont:LOCATION

IBM:ORGANIZATION

Sally:PERSON

Fred:PERSON
```

Using LingPipe for NER

We previously demonstrated the use of LingPipe using regular expressions in the *Using regular expressions for NER* section earlier in this chapter. Here, we will demonstrate how name entity models and the `ExactDictionaryChunker` class are used to perform NER analysis.

Using LingPipe's name entity models

LingPipe has a few named entity models that we can use with chunking. These files consist of a serialized object that can be read from a file and then applied to text. These objects implement the `Chunker` interface. The chunking process results in a series of `Chunking` objects that identify the entities of interest.

A list of the NER models is found in the following table. These models can be downloaded from `http://alias-i.com/lingpipe/web/models.html`:

Genre	Corpus	File
English News	MUC-6	`ne-en-news-muc6.AbstractCharLmRescoringChunker`
English Genes	GeneTag	`ne-en-bio-genetag.HmmChunker`
English Genomics	GENIA	`ne-en-bio-genia.TokenShapeChunker`

We will use the model found in the `ne-en-news-muc6.AbstractCharLmRescoringChunker` file to demonstrate how this class is used. We start with a try-catch block to deal with exceptions as shown in the following example. The file is opened and used with the `AbstractExternalizable` class' static `readObject` method to create an instance of a `Chunker` class. This method will read in the serialized model:

```
try {
    File modelFile = new File(getModelDir(),
        "ne-en-news-muc6.AbstractCharLmRescoringChunker");
    Chunker chunker = (Chunker)
        AbstractExternalizable.readObject(modelFile);
    ...
} catch (IOException | ClassNotFoundException ex) {
    // Handle exception
}
```

The Chunker and Chunking interfaces provide methods that work with a set of chunks of text. Its chunk method returns an object that implements the Chunking instance. The following sequence displays the chunks found in each sentence of the text, as shown here:

```
for (int i = 0; i < sentences.length; ++i) {
    Chunking chunking = chunker.chunk(sentences[i]);
    System.out.println("Chunking=" + chunking);
}
```

The output of this sequence is as follows:

```
Chunking=Joe was the last person to see Fred.   : [0-3:PERSON@-Infinity,
31-35:ORGANIZATION@-Infinity]
```

```
Chunking=He saw him in Boston at McKenzie's pub at 3:00 where he paid
$2.45 for an ale.  : [14-20:LOCATION@-Infinity, 24-32:PERSON@-Infinity]
```

```
Chunking=Joe wanted to go to Vermont for the day to visit a cousin who
works at IBM, but Sally and he had to look for Fred : [0-3:PERSON@-
Infinity, 20-27:ORGANIZATION@-Infinity, 71-74:ORGANIZATION@-Infinity,
109-113:ORGANIZATION@-Infinity]
```

Instead, we can use methods of the Chunk class to extract specific pieces of information as illustrated here. We will replace the previous for statement with the following for-each statement. This calls a displayChunkSet method developed in the *Using LingPipe's RegExChunker class* section earlier in this chapter:

```
for (String sentence : sentences) {
    displayChunkSet(chunker, sentence);
}
```

The output that follows shows the result. However, it does not always match the entity type correctly.

```
Type: PERSON Entity: [Joe] Score: -Infinity
```

```
Type: ORGANIZATION Entity: [Fred] Score: -Infinity
```

```
Type: LOCATION Entity: [Boston] Score: -Infinity
```

```
Type: PERSON Entity: [McKenzie] Score: -Infinity
```

```
Type: PERSON Entity: [Joe] Score: -Infinity
```

```
Type: ORGANIZATION Entity: [Vermont] Score: -Infinity
```

```
Type: ORGANIZATION Entity: [IBM] Score: -Infinity
```

```
Type: ORGANIZATION Entity: [Fred] Score: -Infinity
```

Using the ExactDictionaryChunker class

The ExactDictionaryChunker class provides an easy way to create a dictionary of entities and their types, which can be used to find them later in text. It uses a MapDictionary object to store entries and then the ExactDictionaryChunker class is used to extract chunks based on the dictionary.

The AbstractDictionary interface supports basic operations for entities, categories, and scores. The score is used in the matching process. The MapDictionary and TrieDictionary classes implement the AbstractDictionary interface. The TrieDictionary class stores information using a character trie structure. This approach uses less memory when it is a concern. We will use the MapDictionary class for our example.

To illustrate this approach, we start with a declaration of the MapDictionary class:

```
private MapDictionary<String> dictionary;
```

The dictionary will contain the entities that we are interested in finding. We need to initialize the model as performed in the following initializeDictionary method. The DictionaryEntry constructor used here accepts three arguments:

- String: The name of the entity
- String: The category of the entity
- Double: Represent a score for the entity

The score is used when determining matches. A few entities are declared and added to the dictionary.

```
private static void initializeDictionary() {
    dictionary = new MapDictionary<String>();
    dictionary.addEntry(
        new DictionaryEntry<String>("Joe","PERSON",1.0));
    dictionary.addEntry(
        new DictionaryEntry<String>("Fred","PERSON",1.0));
    dictionary.addEntry(
        new DictionaryEntry<String>("Boston","PLACE",1.0));
    dictionary.addEntry(
        new DictionaryEntry<String>("pub","PLACE",1.0));
    dictionary.addEntry(
        new DictionaryEntry<String>("Vermont","PLACE",1.0));
    dictionary.addEntry(
        new DictionaryEntry<String>("IBM","ORGANIZATION",1.0));
    dictionary.addEntry(
        new DictionaryEntry<String>("Sally","PERSON",1.0));
}
```

An `ExactDictionaryChunker` instance will use this dictionary. The arguments of the `ExactDictionaryChunker` class are detailed here:

- `Dictionary<String>`: It is a dictionary containing the entities
- `TokenizerFactory`: It is a tokenizer used by the chunker
- `boolean`: If it is `true`, the chunker should return all matches
- `boolean`: If it is `true`, matches are case sensitive

Matches can be overlapping. For example, in the phrase "The First National Bank", the entity "bank" could be used by itself or in conjunction with the rest of the phrase. The third parameter determines if all of the matches are returned.

In the following sequence, the dictionary is initialized. We then create an instance of the `ExactDictionaryChunker` class using the Indo-European tokenizer, where we return all matches and ignore the case of the tokens:

```
initializeDictionary();
ExactDictionaryChunker dictionaryChunker
    = new ExactDictionaryChunker(dictionary,
        IndoEuropeanTokenizerFactory.INSTANCE, true, false);
```

The `dictionaryChunker` object is used with each sentence, as shown in the following code sequence. We will use the `displayChunkSet` method as developed in the *Using LingPipe's RegExChunker class* section earlier in this chapter:

```
for (String sentence : sentences) {
    System.out.println("\nTEXT=" + sentence);
    displayChunkSet(dictionaryChunker, sentence);
}
```

On execution, we get the following output:

TEXT=Joe was the last person to see Fred.

Type: PERSON Entity: [Joe] Score: 1.0

Type: PERSON Entity: [Fred] Score: 1.0

TEXT=He saw him in Boston at McKenzie's pub at 3:00 where he paid $2.45 for an ale.

Type: PLACE Entity: [Boston] Score: 1.0

Type: PLACE Entity: [pub] Score: 1.0

```
TEXT=Joe wanted to go to Vermont for the day to visit a cousin who works
at IBM, but Sally and he had to look for Fred

Type: PERSON Entity: [Joe] Score: 1.0

Type: PLACE Entity: [Vermont] Score: 1.0

Type: ORGANIZATION Entity: [IBM] Score: 1.0

Type: PERSON Entity: [Sally] Score: 1.0

Type: PERSON Entity: [Fred] Score: 1.0
```

This does a pretty good job but it requires a lot of effort to create the dictionary for a large vocabulary.

Training a model

We will use OpenNLP to demonstrate how a model is trained. The training file used must:

- Contain marks to demarcate the entities
- Have one sentence per line

We will use the following model file named en-ner-person.train:

```
<START:person> Joe <END> was the last person to see <START:person>
Fred <END>.
He saw him in Boston at McKenzie's pub at 3:00 where he paid $2.45 for
an ale.
<START:person> Joe <END> wanted to go to Vermont for the day to visit
a cousin who works at IBM, but <START:person> Sally <END> and he had
to look for <START:person> Fred <END>.
```

Several methods of this example are capable of throwing exceptions. These statements will be placed in a try-with-resource block as shown here, where the model's output stream is created:

```
try (OutputStream modelOutputStream = new BufferedOutputStream(
        new FileOutputStream(new File("modelFile")));) {
    ...
} catch (IOException ex) {
    // Handle exception
}
```

Within the block, we create an OutputStream<String> object using the PlainTextByLineStream class. This class' constructor takes a FileInputStream instance and returns each line as a String object. The en-ner-person.train file is used as the input file, as shown here. The UTF-8 string refers to the encoding sequence used:

```
ObjectStream<String> lineStream = new PlainTextByLineStream(
    new FileInputStream("en-ner-person.train"), "UTF-8");
```

The lineStream object contains streams that are annotated with tags delineating the entities in the text. These need to be converted to the NameSample objects so that the model can be trained. This conversion is performed by the NameSampleDataStream class as shown here. A NameSample object holds the names of the entities found in the text:

```
ObjectStream<NameSample> sampleStream =
    new NameSampleDataStream(lineStream);
```

The train method can now be executed as follows:

```
TokenNameFinderModel model = NameFinderME.train(
    "en", "person",  sampleStream,
    Collections.<String, Object>emptyMap(), 100, 5);
```

The arguments of the method are as detailed in the following table:

Parameter	Meaning
"en"	Language Code
"person"	Entity type
sampleStream	Sample data
null	Resources
100	The number of iterations
5	The cutoff

The model is then serialized to an output file:

```
model.serialize(modelOutputStream);
```

The output of this sequence is as follows. It has been shortened to conserve space. Basic information about the model creation is detailed:

```
Indexing events using cutoff of 5


  Computing event counts...   done. 53 events
  Indexing...   done.
Sorting and merging events... done. Reduced 53 events to 46.
Done indexing.
Incorporating indexed data for training...
done.
  Number of Event Tokens: 46
      Number of Outcomes: 2
    Number of Predicates: 34
...done.
Computing model parameters ...
Performing 100 iterations.
  1:   ... loglikelihood=-36.73680056967707   0.05660377358490566
  2:   ... loglikelihood=-17.499660626361216   0.9433962264150944
  3:   ... loglikelihood=-13.216835449617108   0.9433962264150944
  4:   ... loglikelihood=-11.461783667999262   0.9433962264150944
  5:   ... loglikelihood=-10.380239416084963   0.9433962264150944
  6:   ... loglikelihood=-9.570622475692486   0.9433962264150944
  7:   ... loglikelihood=-8.919945779143012   0.9433962264150944
  ...
  99:   ... loglikelihood=-3.513810438211968   0.9622641509433962
 100:   ... loglikelihood=-3.507213816708068   0.9622641509433962
```

Evaluating a model

The model can be evaluated using the `TokenNameFinderEvaluator` class. The evaluation process uses marked up sample text to perform the evaluation. For this simple example, a file called `en-ner-person.eval` was created that contained the following text:

```
<START:person> Bill <END> went to the farm to see <START:person> Sally
<END>.
Unable to find <START:person> Sally <END> he went to town.
There he saw <START:person> Fred <END> who had seen <START:person>
Sally <END> at the book store with <START:person> Mary <END>.
```

The following code is used to perform the evaluation. The previous model is used as the argument of the `TokenNameFinderEvaluator` constructor. A `NameSampleDataStream` instance is created based on the evaluation file. The `TokenNameFinderEvaluator` class' `evaluate` method performs the evaluation:

```
TokenNameFinderEvaluator evaluator =
    new TokenNameFinderEvaluator(new NameFinderME(model));
lineStream = new PlainTextByLineStream(
    new FileInputStream("en-ner-person.eval"), "UTF-8");
sampleStream = new NameSampleDataStream(lineStream);
evaluator.evaluate(sampleStream);
```

To determine how well the model worked with the evaluation data, the `getFMeasure` method is executed. The results are then displayed:

```
FMeasure result = evaluator.getFMeasure();
System.out.println(result.toString());
```

The following output displays the precision, recall, and F-measure. It indicates that 50 percent of the entities found exactly match the evaluation data. The recall is the percentage of entities defined in the corpus that were found in the same location. The performance measure is the harmonic mean and is defined as: *F1 = 2 * Precision * Recall / (Recall + Precision)*

Precision: 0.5

Recall: 0.25

F-Measure: 0.3333333333333333

The data and evaluation sets should be much larger to create a better model. The intent here was to demonstrate the basic approach used to train and evaluate a POS model.

Summary

NER involves detecting entities and then classifying them. Common categories include names, locations, and things. This is an important task that many applications use to support searching, resolving references, and finding the meaning of the text. The process is frequently used in downstream tasks.

We investigated several techniques for performing NER. Regular expressions is one approach that is supported by both core Java classes and NLP APIs. This technique is useful for many applications and there are a large number of regular expression libraries available.

Dictionary-based approaches are also possible and work well for some applications. However, they require considerable effort to populate at times. We used LingPipe's `MapDictionary` class to illustrate this approach.

Trained models can also be used to perform NER. We examined several of these and demonstrated how to train a model using the Open NLP `NameFinderME` class. This process was very similar to the earlier training processes.

In the next chapter, we will learn how to detect parts of speech such as nouns, adjectives, and prepositions.

5
Detecting Part of Speech

Previously, we identified parts of text such as people, places, and things. In this chapter, we will investigate the process of finding POS. These are the parts that we recognize in English as the grammatical elements, such as nouns and verbs. We will find that the context of the word is an important aspect of determining what type of word it is.

We will examine the tagging process, which essentially assigns a POS to a tag. This process is at the heart of detecting POS. We will briefly discuss why tagging is important and then examine the various factors that makes detecting POS difficult. Various NLP APIs are then used to illustrate the tagging process. We will also demonstrate how to train a model to address specialized text.

The tagging process

Tagging is the process of assigning a description to a token or a portion of text. This description is called a **tag**. **POS tagging** is the process of assigning a POS tag to a token. These tags are normally tags such as noun, verb, and adjective.

For example, consider the following sentence:

"The cow jumped over the moon."

For many of these initial examples, we will illustrate the result of a POS tagger using the OpenNLP tagger to be discussed in *Using OpenNLP POS taggers*, later in this chapter. If we use that tagger with the previous example, we will get the following results. Notice that the words are followed by a forward slash and then their POS tag. These tags will be explained shortly:

```
The/DT cow/NN jumped/VBD over/IN the/DT moon./NN
```

Words can potentially have more than one tag associated with them depending on their context. For example, the word "saw" could be a noun or a verb. When a word can be classified into different categories, information such as its position, words in its vicinity, or similar information are used to probabilistically determine the appropriate category. For example, if a word is preceded by a determiner and followed by a noun, then tag the word as an adjective.

The general tagging process consists of tokenizing the text, determining possible tags, and resolving ambiguous tags. Algorithms are used to perform POS identification (tagging). There are two general approaches:

- **Rule-based**: Rule-based taggers uses a set of rules and a dictionary of words and possible tags. The rules are used when a word has multiple tags. Rules often use the previous and/or following words to select a tag.

- **Stochastic**: Stochastic taggers use is either based on the Markov model or are cue-based, which uses either decision trees or maximum entropy. Markov models are finite state machines where each state has two probability distributions. Its objective is to find the optimal sequence of tags for a sentence. **Hidden Markov Models (HMM)** are also used. In these models, the state transitions are not visible.

A maximum entropy tagger uses statistics to determine the POS for a word and often uses a corpus to train a model. A corpus is a collection of words marked up with POS tags. Corpora exist for a number of languages. These take a lot of effort to develop. Frequently used corpora include the Penn Treebank (`http://www.cis.upenn.edu/~treebank/`) or Brown Corpus (`http://www.essex.ac.uk/linguistics/external/clmt/w3c/corpus_ling/content/corpora/list/private/brown/brown.html`).

A sample from the Penn Treebank corpus, which illustrates POS markup, is as follows:

```
Well/UH what/WP do/VBP you/PRP think/VB about/IN
the/DT idea/NN of/IN ,/, uh/UH ,/, kids/NNS having/VBG
to/TO do/VB public/JJ service/NN work/NN for/IN a/DT
year/NN ?/.
```

There are traditionally nine parts of speech in English: noun, verb, article, adjective, preposition, pronoun, adverb, conjunction, and interjection. However, a more complete analysis often requires additional categories and subcategories. There have been as many as 150 different parts of speech identified. In some situations, it may be necessary to create new tags. A short list is shown in the following table.

These are the tags we use frequently in this chapter:

Part	Meaning
NN	Noun, singular or mass
DT	Determiner
VB	Verb, base form
VBD	Verb, past tense
VBZ	Verb, third person singular present
IN	Preposition or subordinating conjunction
NNP	Proper noun, singular
TO	to
JJ	Adjective

A more comprehensive list is shown in the following table. This list is adapted from `https://www.ling.upenn.edu/courses/Fall_2003/ling001/penn_treebank_pos.html`. The complete list of The University of Pennsylvania (Penn) Treebank Tagset can be found at `http://www.comp.leeds.ac.uk/ccalas/tagsets/upenn.html`. A set of tags is referred to as a **tag set**.

Tag	Description	Tag	Description
CC	Coordinating conjunction	PRP$	Possessive pronoun
CD	Cardinal number	RB	Adverb
DT	Determiner	RBR	Adverb, comparative
EX	Existential there	RBS	Adverb, superlative
FW	Foreign word	RP	Particle
IN	Preposition or subordinating conjunction	SYM	Symbol
JJ	Adjective	TO	to
JJR	Adjective, comparative	UH	Interjection
JJS	Adjective, superlative	VB	Verb, base form
LS	List item marker	VBD	Verb, past tense
MD	Modal	VBG	Verb, gerund or present participle
NN	Noun, singular or mass	VBN	Verb, past participle
NNS	Noun, plural	VBP	Verb, non-third person singular present

Tag	Description	Tag	Description
NNP	Proper noun, singular	VBZ	Verb, third person singular present
NNPS	Proper noun, plural	WDT	Wh-determiner
PDT	Predeterminer	WP	Wh-pronoun
POS	Possessive ending	WP$	Possessive wh-pronoun
PRP	Personal pronoun	WRB	Wh-adverb

The development of a manual corpus is labor intensive. However, some statistical techniques have been developed to create corpora. A number of corpora are available. One of the first ones was the Brown Corpus (`http://clu.uni.no/icame/manuals/BROWN/INDEX.HTM`). Newer ones include the British National Corpus (`http://www.natcorp.ox.ac.uk/corpus/index.xml`), with over 100 million words, and the American National Corpus (`http://www.anc.org/`). A list of corpora can be found at `http://en.wikipedia.org/wiki/List_of_text_corpora`.

Importance of POS taggers

Proper tagging of a sentence can enhance the quality of downstream processing tasks. If we know that "sue" is a verb and not a noun, then this can assist in the correct relationship among tokens. Determining the POS, phrases, clauses, and any relationship between them is called **parsing**. This is in contrast to tokenization where we are only interested in identifying "word" elements and we are not concerned about their meaning.

POS tagging is used for many downstream processes such as question analysis and analyzing the sentiment of text. Some social media sites are frequently interested in assessing the sentiment of their clients' communication. Text indexing will frequently use POS data. Speech processing can use tags to help decide how to pronounce words.

What makes POS difficult?

There are many aspects of a language that can make POS tagging difficult. Most English words will have two or more tags associated with them. A dictionary is not always sufficient to determine a word's POS. For example, the meaning of words like "bill" and "force" are dependent on their context. The following sentence demonstrates how they can both be used in the same sentence as nouns and verbs.

"Bill used the force to force the manger to tear the bill in two."

Using the OpenNLP tagger with this sentence produces the following output:

```
Bill/NNP used/VBD the/DT force/NN to/TO force/VB the/DT manger/NN to/TO
tear/VB the/DT bill/NN in/IN two./PRP$
```

The use of **textese**, a combination of different forms of text including abbreviations, hashtags, emoticons, and slang, in communications mediums such as tweets and text makes it more difficult to tag sentences. For example, the following message is difficult to tag:

"AFAIK she H8 cth! BTW had a GR8 tym at the party BBIAM."

Its equivalent is:

"As far as I know, she hates cleaning the house! By the way, had a great time at the party. Be back in a minute."

Using the OpenNLP tagger, we will get the following output:

```
AFAIK/NNS she/PRP H8/CD cth!/.
```

```
BTW/NNP had/VBD a/DT GR8/CD tym/NN at/IN the/DT party/NN BBIAM./.
```

In the *Using the MaxentTagger class to tag textese* section later in this chapter, we will provide a demonstration of how LingPipe can handle textese. A short list of textese is given in the following table:

Phrase	Textese	Phrase	Textese
As far as I know	AFAIK	By the way	BTW
Away from keyboard	AFK	You're on your own	YOYO
Thanks	THNX or THX	As soon as possible	ASAP
Today	2day	What do you mean by that	WDYMBT
Before	B4	Be back in a minute	BBIAM
See you	C U	Can't	CNT
Haha	hh	Later	l8R
Laughing out loud	LOL	On the other hand	OTOH
Rolling on the floor laughing	ROFL or ROTFL	I don't know	IDK
Great	GR8	Cleaning the house	CTH
At the moment	ATM	In my humble opinion	IMHO

Although there are several list of textese, a large list can be found at `http://www.ukrainecalling.com/textspeak.aspx`.

Tokenization is an important step in the POS tagging process. If the tokens are not split properly, we can get erroneous results. There are several other potential problems including:

- If we use lowercase, then words such as "sam" can be confused with the person or for the System for Award Management (www.sam.gov)
- We have to take into account contractions such as "can't" and recognize that different characters may be used for the apostrophe
- Although phrases such as "vice versa" can be treated as a unit, it has been used for a band in England, the title of a novel, and as the title of a magazine
- We can't ignore hyphenated words such as "first-cut" and "prime-cut" that have meanings different from their individual use
- Some words have embedded numbers such as iPhone 5S
- Special character sequences such as a URL or e-mail address also need to be handled

Some words are found embedded in quotes or parentheses, which can make their meaning confusing. Consider the following example:

"Whether "Blue" was correct or not (it's not) is debatable."

"Blue" could refer to the color blue or conceivably the nickname of a person. The output of the tagger for this sentence is as follows:

```
Whether/IN "Blue"/NNP was/VBD correct/JJ or/CC not/RB (it's/JJ not)/NN
is/VBZ debatable/VBG
```

Using the NLP APIs

We will demonstrate POS tagging using OpenNLP, Stanford API, and LingPipe. Each of the examples will use the following sentence. It is the first sentence of *Chapter 5, At A Venture* of *Twenty Thousands Leagues Under the Sea* by *Jules Verne*:

```
private String[] sentence = {"The", "voyage", "of", "the",
    "Abraham", "Lincoln", "was", "for", "a", "long", "time", "marked",
    "by", "no", "special", "incident."};
```

The text to be processed may not always be defined in this fashion. Sometimes the sentence will be available as a single string:

```
String theSentence = "The voyage of the Abraham Lincoln was for a "
    + "long time marked by no special incident.";
```

We might need to convert a string to an array of strings. There are numerous techniques for converting this string to an array of words. The following tokenizeSentence method performs this operation:

```
public String[] tokenizeSentence(String sentence) {
    String words[] = sentence.split("S+");
    return words;
}
```

The following code demonstrates the use of this method:

```
String words[] = tokenizeSentence(theSentence);
for(String word : words) {
    System.out.print(word + " ");
}
System.out.println();
```

The output is as follows:

The voyage of the Abraham Lincoln was for a long time marked by no special incident.

Alternately, we could use a tokenizer such as OpenNLP's WhitespaceTokenizer class, as shown here:

```
String words[] =
    WhitespaceTokenizer.INSTANCE.tokenize(sentence);
```

Using OpenNLP POS taggers

OpenNLP provides several classes in support of POS tagging. We will demonstrate how to use the POSTaggerME class to perform basic tagging and the ChunkerME class to perform chunking. Chunking involves grouping related words according to their types. This can provide additional insight into the structure of a sentence. We will also examine the creation and use of a POSDictionary instance.

Using the OpenNLP POSTaggerME class for POS taggers

The OpenNLP POSTaggerME class uses maximum entropy to process the tags. The tagger determines the type of tag based on the word itself and the word's context. Any given word may have multiple tags associated with it. The tagger uses a probability model to determine the specific tag to be assigned.

POS models are loaded from a file. The en-pos-maxent.bin model is used frequently and is based on the Penn TreeBank tag set. Various pretrained POS models for OpenNLP can be found at http://opennlp.sourceforge.net/models-1.5/.

We start with a try-catch block to handle any IOException that might be generated when loading a model, as shown here.

We use the en-pos-maxent.bin file for the model:

```
try (InputStream modelIn = new FileInputStream(
    new File(getModelDir(), "en-pos-maxent.bin"));) {
    ...
}
catch (IOException e) {
    // Handle exceptions
}
```

Next, create the POSModel and POSTaggerME instances as shown here:

```
POSModel model = new POSModel(modelIn);
POSTaggerME tagger = new POSTaggerME(model);
```

The tag method can now be applied to the tagger using the text to be processed as its argument:

```
String tags[] = tagger.tag(sentence);
```

The words and their tags are then displayed as shown here:

```
for (int i = 0; i<sentence.length; i++) {
    System.out.print(sentence[i] + "/" + tags[i] + " ");
}
```

The output is as follows. Each word is followed by its type:

```
The/DT voyage/NN of/IN the/DT Abraham/NNP Lincoln/NNP was/VBD for/IN a/DT
long/JJ time/NN marked/VBN by/IN no/DT special/JJ incident./NN
```

With any sentence, there may be more than one possible assignment of tags to words. The topKSequences method will return a set of sequences based on their probability of being correct. In the next code sequence, the topKSequences method is executed using the sentence variable and then displayed:

```
Sequence topSequences[] = tagger.topKSequences(sentence);
for (inti = 0; i<topSequences.length; i++) {
    System.out.println(topSequences[i]);
}
```

Its output follows in which the first number represents a weighted score and the tags within the brackets are the sequence of tags scored:

```
-0.5563571615737618 [DT, NN, IN, DT, NNP, NNP, VBD, IN, DT, JJ, NN, VBN,
IN, DT, JJ, NN]

-2.9886144610050907 [DT, NN, IN, DT, NNP, NNP, VBD, IN, DT, JJ, NN, VBN,
IN, DT, JJ, .]

-3.771930515521527 [DT, NN, IN, DT, NNP, NNP, VBD, IN, DT, JJ, NN, VBN,
IN, DT, NN, NN]
```

 Ensure that you include the correct Sequence class. For this example, use import opennlp.tools.util.Sequence;

The Sequence class has several methods, as detailed in the following table:

Method	Meaning
getOutcomes	Returns a list of strings representing the tags for the sentence
getProbs	Returns an array of double variables representing the probability for each tag in the sequence
getScore	Returns a weighted value for the sequence

In the following sequence, we use several of these methods to demonstrate what they do. For each sequence, the tags and their probability are displayed, separated by a forward slash:

```
for (int i = 0; i<topSequences.length; i++) {
    List<String> outcomes = topSequences[i].getOutcomes();
    double probabilities[] = topSequences[i].getProbs();
    for (int j = 0; j <outcomes.size(); j++) {
        System.out.printf("%s/%5.3f ",outcomes.get(j),
        probabilities[j]);
```

```
    }
    System.out.println();
  }
  System.out.println();
```

The output is as follows. Each pair of lines represents one sequence where the output has been wrapped:

```
DT/0.992 NN/0.990 IN/0.989 DT/0.990 NNP/0.996 NNP/0.991 VBD/0.994
IN/0.996 DT/0.996 JJ/0.991 NN/0.994 VBN/0.860 IN/0.985 DT/0.960 JJ/0.919
NN/0.832

DT/0.992 NN/0.990 IN/0.989 DT/0.990 NNP/0.996 NNP/0.991 VBD/0.994
IN/0.996 DT/0.996 JJ/0.991 NN/0.994 VBN/0.860 IN/0.985 DT/0.960 JJ/0.919
./0.073

DT/0.992 NN/0.990 IN/0.989 DT/0.990 NNP/0.996 NNP/0.991 VBD/0.994
IN/0.996 DT/0.996 JJ/0.991 NN/0.994 VBN/0.860 IN/0.985 DT/0.960 NN/0.073
NN/0.419
```

Using OpenNLP chunking

The process of chunking involves breaking a sentence into parts or chunks. These chunks can then be annotated with tags. We will use the ChunkerME class to illustrate how this is accomplished. This class uses a model loaded into a ChunkerModel instance. The ChunkerME class' chunk method performs the actual chunking process. We will also examine the use of the chunkAsSpans method to return information about the span of these chunks. This allows us to see how long a chunk is and what elements make up the chunk.

We will use the en-pos-maxent.bin file to create a model for the POSTaggerME instance. We need to use this instance to tag the text as we did in the *Using OpenNLP POSTaggerME class for POS taggers* section earlier in this chapter. We will also use the en-chunker.bin file to create a ChunkerModel instance to be used with the ChunkerME instance.

These models are created using input streams, as shown in the following example.

We use a try-with-resources block to open and close files and to deal with any exceptions that may be thrown:

```
try (
        InputStream posModelStream = new FileInputStream(
            getModelDir() + "\\en-pos-maxent.bin");
```

```
        InputStream chunkerStream = new FileInputStream(
            getModelDir() + "\\en-chunker.bin");) {
    ...
} catch (IOException ex) {
    // Handle exceptions
}
```

The following code sequence creates and uses a tagger to find the POS of the sentence. The sentence and its tags are then displayed:

```
POSModel model = new POSModel(posModelStream);
POSTaggerME tagger = new POSTaggerME(model);

String tags[] = tagger.tag(sentence);
for(int i=0; i<tags.length; i++) {
    System.out.print(sentence[i] + "/" + tags[i] + " ");
}
System.out.println();
```

The output is as follows. We have shown this output so that it will be clear how the chunker works:

The/DT voyage/NN of/IN the/DT Abraham/NNP Lincoln/NNP was/VBD for/IN a/DT long/JJ time/NN marked/VBN by/IN no/DT special/JJ incident./NN

A `ChunkerModel` instance is created using the input stream. From this, the `ChunkerME` instance is created followed by the use of the `chunk` method as shown here. The `chunk` method will use the sentence's token and its tags to create an array of strings. Each string will hold information about the token and its chunk:

```
ChunkerModel chunkerModel = new
    ChunkerModel(chunkerStream);
ChunkerME chunkerME = new ChunkerME(chunkerModel);
String result[] = chunkerME.chunk(sentence, tags);
```

Each token in the `results` array and its chunk tag are displayed as shown here:

```
for (int i = 0; i < result.length; i++) {
    System.out.println("[" + sentence[i] + "] " + result[i]);
}
```

The output is as follows. The token is enclosed in brackets followed by the chunk tag. These tags are explained in the following table:

First Part	
B	Beginning of a tag
I	Continuation of a tag
E	End of a tag (will not appear if tag is one word long)
Second Part	
NP	Noun chunk
VB	Verb chunk

Multiple words are grouped together such as "The voyage" and "the Abraham Lincoln".

```
[The] B-NP

[voyage] I-NP

[of] B-PP

[the] B-NP

[Abraham] I-NP

[Lincoln] I-NP

[was] B-VP

[for] B-PP

[a] B-NP

[long] I-NP

[time] I-NP

[marked] B-VP

[by] B-PP

[no] B-NP

[special] I-NP

[incident.] I-NP
```

If we are interested in getting more detailed information about the chunks, we can use the `ChunkerME` class' `chunkAsSpans` method. This method returns an array of `Span` objects. Each object represents one span found in the text.

There are several other `ChunkerME` class methods available. Here, we will illustrate the use of the `getType`, `getStart`, and `getEnd` methods. The `getType` method returns the second part of the chunk tag, and the `getStart` and `getEnd` methods return the beginning and ending index of the tokens, respectively, in the original `sentence` array. The `length` method returns the length of the span in number of tokens.

In the following sequence, the `chunkAsSpans` method is executed using the `sentence` and `tags` arrays. The `spans` array is then displayed. The outer for loop processes one `Span` object at a time displaying the basic span information. The inner for loop displays the spanned text enclosed within brackets:

```
Span[] spans = chunkerME.chunkAsSpans(sentence, tags);
for (Span span : spans) {
    System.out.print("Type: " + span.getType() + " - "
        + " Begin: " + span.getStart()
        + " End:" + span.getEnd()
        + " Length: " + span.length() + "  [");
    for (int j = span.getStart(); j < span.getEnd(); j++) {
        System.out.print(sentence[j] + " ");
    }
    System.out.println("]");
}
```

The following output clearly shows the span type, its position in the `sentence` array, its length, and then the actual spanned text:

```
Type: NP -  Begin: 0 End:2 Length: 2   [The voyage ]
Type: PP -  Begin: 2 End:3 Length: 1   [of ]
Type: NP -  Begin: 3 End:6 Length: 3   [the Abraham Lincoln ]
Type: VP -  Begin: 6 End:7 Length: 1   [was ]
Type: PP -  Begin: 7 End:8 Length: 1   [for ]
Type: NP -  Begin: 8 End:11 Length: 3   [a long time ]
Type: VP -  Begin: 11 End:12 Length: 1  [marked ]
Type: PP -  Begin: 12 End:13 Length: 1  [by ]
Type: NP -  Begin: 13 End:16 Length: 3  [no special incident. ]
```

Using the POSDictionary class

A tag dictionary specifies what are the valid tags for a word. This can prevent a tag from being applied inappropriately to a word. In addition, some search algorithms execute faster since they do not have to consider other less probable tags.

In this section, we will demonstrate how to:

- Obtain the tag dictionary for a tagger
- Determine what tags a word has
- Show how to change the tags for a word
- Add a new tag dictionary to a new tagger factory

As with the previous example, we will use a try-with-resources block to open our input streams for the POS model and then create our model and tagger factory, as shown here:

```
try (InputStream modelIn = new FileInputStream(
        new File(getModelDir(), "en-pos-maxent.bin"));) {
    POSModel model = new POSModel(modelIn);
    POSTaggerFactory posTaggerFactory = model.getFactory();
    ...
} catch (IOException e) {
    //Handle exceptions
}
```

Obtaining the tag dictionary for a tagger

We used the POSModel class' getFactory method to get a POSTaggerFactory instance. We will use its getTagDictionary method to obtain its TagDictionary instance. This is illustrated here:

```
MutableTagDictionary tagDictionary =
    (MutableTagDictionary)posTaggerFactory.getTagDictionary();
```

The MutableTagDictionary interface extends the TagDictionary interface. The TagDictionary interface possesses a getTags method, and the MutableTagDictionary interface adds a put method that allows tags to be added to the dictionary. These interfaces are implemented by the POSDictionary class.

Determining a word's tags

To obtain the tags for a given word, use the `getTags` method. This returns an array of tags represented by strings. The tags are then displayed as shown here:

```
String tags[] = tagDictionary.getTags("force");
for (String tag : tags) {
    System.out.print("/" + tag);
}
System.out.println();
```

The output is as follows:

/NN/VBP/VB

This means that the word "force" can be interpreted in three different ways.

Changing a word's tags

The `MutableTagDictionary` interface's `put` method allows us to add tags to a word. The method has two arguments: the word, and its new tags. The method returns an array containing the previous tags.

In the following example, we replace the old tags with a new tag. The old tags are then displayed.

```
String oldTags[] = tagDictionary.put("force", "newTag");
for (String tag : oldTags) {
    System.out.print("/" + tag);
}
System.out.println();
```

The following output lists the old tags for the word.

/NN/VBP/VB

These tags have been replaced by the new tag as demonstrated here where the current tags are displayed:

```
tags = tagDictionary.getTags("force");
for (String tag : tags) {
    System.out.print("/" + tag);
}
System.out.println();
```

All we get is the following:

/newTag

To retain the old tags we will need to create an array of strings to hold the old and the new tags and then use the array as the second argument of the put method as shown here:

```
String newTags[] = new String[tags.length+1];
for (int i=0; i<tags.length; i++) {
    newTags[i] = tags[i];
}
newTags[tags.length] = "newTag";
oldTags = tagDictionary.put("force", newTags);
```

If we redisplay the current tags as shown here, we can see that the old tags have been retained and the new one added:

/NN/VBP/VB/newTag

When adding tags, be careful and assign the tags in the proper order as it will influence which tag is assigned.

Adding a new tag dictionary

A new tag dictionary can be added to a POSTaggerFactory instance. We will illustrate this process by creating a new POSTaggerFactory and then adding the tagDictionary we developed earlier. First, we create a new factory using the default constructor as shown next. This is followed by calling the setTagDictionary method against the new factory.

```
POSTaggerFactory newFactory = new POSTaggerFactory();
newFactory.setTagDictionary(tagDictionary);
```

To confirm that the tag dictionary has been added, we display the tags for the word "force" as shown here:

```
tags = newFactory.getTagDictionary().getTags("force");
for (String tag : tags) {
    System.out.print("/" + tag);
}
System.out.println();
```

The tags are the same as shown here:

/NN/VBP/VB/newTag

Creating a dictionary from a file

If we need to create a new dictionary, then one approach is to create an XML file containing all of the words and their tags, and then create the dictionary from the file. OpenNLP supports this approach with the POSDictionary class' create method.

The XML file consists of the dictionary root element followed by a series of entry elements. The entry element uses the tags attribute to specify the tags for the word. The word is contained within the entry element as a token element. A simple example using two words stored in the file dictionary.txt is as follows:

```
<dictionary case_sensitive="false">
    <entry tags="JJ VB">
        <token>strong</token>
    </entry>
    <entry tags="NN VBP VB">
        <token>force</token>
    </entry>
</dictionary>
```

To create the dictionary, we use the create method based on an input stream as shown here:

```
try (InputStream dictionaryIn =
        new FileInputStream(new File("dictionary.txt"));) {
    POSDictionary dictionary =
    POSDictionary.create(dictionaryIn);
    ...
} catch (IOException e) {
    // Handle exceptions
}
```

The POSDictionary class has an iterator method that returns an iterator object. Its next method returns a string for each word in the dictionary. We can use these methods to display the contents of the dictionary, as shown here:

```
Iterator<String> iterator = dictionary.iterator();
while (iterator.hasNext()) {
    String entry = iterator.next();
    String tags[] = dictionary.getTags(entry);
    System.out.print(entry + " ");
    for (String tag : tags) {
        System.out.print("/" + tag);
    }
    System.out.println();
}
```

The output that follows displays what we can expect:

```
strong /JJ/VB
force /NN/VBP/VB
```

Using Stanford POS taggers

In this section, we will examine two different approaches supported by the Stanford API to perform tagging. The first technique uses the MaxentTagger class. As its name implies, it uses maximum entropy to find the POS. We will also use this class to demonstrate a model designed to handle textese-type text. The second approach will use the pipeline approach with annotators. The English taggers use the Penn Treebank English POS tag set.

Using Stanford MaxentTagger

The MaxentTagger class uses a model to perform the tagging task. There are a number of models that come bundled with the API, all with the file extension .tagger. They include English, Chinese, Arabic, French, and German models. The English models are listed here. The prefix, wsj, refers to models based on the Wall Street Journal. The other terms refer to techniques used to train the model. These concepts are not covered here:

- wsj-0-18-bidirectional-distsim.tagger
- wsj-0-18-bidirectional-nodistsim.tagger
- wsj-0-18-caseless-left3words-distsim.tagger
- wsj-0-18-left3words-distsim.tagger
- wsj-0-18-left3words-nodistsim.tagger
- english-bidirectional-distsim.tagger
- english-caseless-left3words-distsim.tagger
- english-left3words-distsim.tagger

The example reads in a series of sentences from a file. Each sentence is then processed and various ways of accessing and displaying the words and tags are illustrated.

We start with a try-with-resources block to deal with IO exceptions as shown here. The wsj-0-18-bidirectional-distsim.tagger file is used to create an instance of the MaxentTagger class.

A `List` instance of `List` instances of `HasWord` objects is created using the `MaxentTagger` class' `tokenizeText` method. The sentences are read in from the file `sentences.txt`. The `HasWord` interface represents words and contains two methods: a `setWord` and a `word` method. The latter method returns a word as a string. Each sentence is represented by a `List` instance of `HasWord` objects:

```
try {
    MaxentTagger tagger = new MaxentTagger(getModelDir() +
        "//wsj-0-18-bidirectional-distsim.tagger");
    List<List<HasWord>> sentences = MaxentTagger.tokenizeText(
        new BufferedReader(new FileReader("sentences.txt")));
    ...
} catch (FileNotFoundException ex) {
    // Handle exceptions
}
```

The `sentences.txt` file contains the first four sentences of *Chapter 5, At A Venture* of the book *Twenty Thousands Leagues Under the Sea*:

```
The voyage of the Abraham Lincoln was for a long time marked by no
special incident.
But one circumstance happened which showed the wonderful dexterity of
Ned Land, and proved what confidence we might place in him.
The 30th of June, the frigate spoke some American whalers, from whom
we learned that they knew nothing about the narwhal.
But one of them, the captain of the Monroe, knowing that Ned Land had
shipped on board the Abraham Lincoln, begged for his help in chasing a
whale they had in sight.
```

A loop is added to process each sentence of the `sentences` list. The `tagSentence` method returns a `List` instance of `TaggedWord` objects as shown next. The `TaggedWord` class implements the `HasWord` interface and adds a `tag` method that returns the tag associated with the word. As shown here, the `toString` method is used to display each sentence:

```
List<TaggedWord> taggedSentence =
    tagger.tagSentence(sentence);
for (List<HasWord> sentence : sentences) {
    List<TaggedWord> taggedSentence=
        tagger.tagSentence(sentence);
    System.out.println(taggedSentence);
}
```

The output is as follows:

```
[The/DT, voyage/NN, of/IN, the/DT, Abraham/NNP, Lincoln/NNP, was/VBD,
for/IN, a/DT, long/JJ, --- time/NN, marked/VBN, by/IN, no/DT, special/JJ,
incident/NN, ./.]
  [But/CC, one/CD, circumstance/NN, happened/VBD, which/WDT, showed/VBD,
the/DT, wonderful/JJ, dexterity/NN, of/IN, Ned/NNP, Land/NNP, ,/,, and/
CC, proved/VBD, what/WP, confidence/NN, we/PRP, might/MD, place/VB, in/
IN, him/PRP, ./.]
[The/DT, 30th/JJ, of/IN, June/NNP, ,/,, the/DT, frigate/NN, spoke/
VBD, some/DT, American/JJ, whalers/NNS, ,/,, from/IN, whom/WP, we/PRP,
learned/VBD, that/IN, they/PRP, knew/VBD, nothing/NN, about/IN, the/DT,
narwhal/NN, ./.]
[But/CC, one/CD, of/IN, them/PRP, ,/,, the/DT, captain/NN, of/IN, the/
DT, Monroe/NNP, ,/,, knowing/VBG, that/IN, Ned/NNP, Land/NNP, had/VBD,
shipped/VBN, on/IN, board/NN, the/DT, Abraham/NNP, Lincoln/NNP, ,/,,
begged/VBN, for/IN, his/PRP$, help/NN, in/IN, chasing/VBG, a/DT, whale/
NN, they/PRP, had/VBD, in/IN, sight/NN, ./.]
```

Alternately, we can use the `Sentence` class' `listToString` method to convert the tagged sentence to a simple `String` object.

A value of `false` for its second parameter is used by the `toString` method of the `HasWord` to create the resulting string, as shown here:

```
List<TaggedWord> taggedSentence =
    tagger.tagSentence(sentence);
for (List<HasWord> sentence : sentences) {
    List<TaggedWord> taggedSentence=
        tagger.tagSentence(sentence);
    System.out.println(Sentence.listToString(taggedSentence, false));
}
```

This produces a more aesthetically pleasing output:

```
The/DT voyage/NN of/IN the/DT Abraham/NNP Lincoln/NNP was/VBD for/IN a/DT
long/JJ time/NN marked/VBN by/IN no/DT special/JJ incident/NN ./.
But/CC one/CD circumstance/NN happened/VBD which/WDT showed/VBD the/DT
wonderful/JJ dexterity/NN of/IN Ned/NNP Land/NNP ,/, and/CC proved/VBD
what/WP confidence/NN we/PRP might/MD place/VB in/IN him/PRP ./.
The/DT 30th/JJ of/IN June/NNP ,/, the/DT frigate/NN spoke/VBD some/DT
American/JJ whalers/NNS ,/, from/IN whom/WP we/PRP learned/VBD that/IN
they/PRP knew/VBD nothing/NN about/IN the/DT narwhal/NN ./.
But/CC one/CD of/IN them/PRP ,/, the/DT captain/NN of/IN the/DT Monroe/
NNP ,/, knowing/VBG that/IN Ned/NNP Land/NNP had/VBD shipped/VBN on/IN
board/NN the/DT Abraham/NNP Lincoln/NNP ,/, begged/VBN for/IN his/PRP$
help/NN in/IN chasing/VBG a/DT whale/NN they/PRP had/VBD in/IN sight/NN
./.
```

We can use the following code sequence to produce the same results. The `word` and `tag` methods extract the words and their tags:

```
List<TaggedWord> taggedSentence =
    tagger.tagSentence(sentence);
for (TaggedWord taggedWord : taggedSentence) {
    System.out.print(taggedWord.word() + "/" +
        taggedWord.tag() + " ");
}
System.out.println();
```

If we are only interested in finding specific occurrences of a given tag, we can use a sequence such as the following, which will list only the singular nouns (NN):

```
List<TaggedWord> taggedSentence =
    tagger.tagSentence(sentence);
for (TaggedWord taggedWord : taggedSentence) {
    if (taggedWord.tag().startsWith("NN")) {
        System.out.print(taggedWord.word() + " ");
    }
}
System.out.println();
```

The singular nouns are displayed for each sentence as shown here:

`NN Tagged: voyage Abraham Lincoln time incident`

`NN Tagged: circumstance dexterity Ned Land confidence`

`NN Tagged: June frigate whalers nothing narwhal`

`NN Tagged: captain Monroe Ned Land board Abraham Lincoln help whale sight`

Using the MaxentTagger class to tag textese

We can use a different model to handle twitter text that may include textese. The GATE (`https://gate.ac.uk/wiki/twitter-postagger.html`) has developed a model for twitter text. The model is used here to process textese:

```
MaxentTagger tagger = new MaxentTagger(getModelDir()
    + "//gate-EN-twitter.model");
```

Here, we use the `MaxentTagger` class' `tagString` method from the *What makes POS difficult?* section earlier in this chapter to process the textese:

```
System.out.println(tagger.tagString("AFAIK she H8 cth!"));
System.out.println(tagger.tagString(
    "BTW had a GR8 tym at the party BBIAM."));
```

The output will be as follows:

```
AFAIK_NNP she_PRP H8_VBP cth!_NN

BTW_UH had_VBD a_DT GR8_NNP tym_NNP at_IN the_DT party_NN BBIAM._NNP
```

Using Stanford pipeline to perform tagging

We have used the Stanford pipeline in several previous examples. In this example, we will use the Stanford pipeline to extract POS tags. As with our previous Stanford examples, we create a pipeline based on a set of annotators: tokenize, ssplit, and pos.

These will tokenize, split the text into sentences, and then find the POS tags:

```
Properties props = new Properties();
props.put("annotators", "tokenize, ssplit, pos");
StanfordCoreNLP pipeline = new StanfordCoreNLP(props);
```

To process the text, we will use the theSentence variable as input to Annotator. The pipeline's annotate method is then invoked as shown here:

```
Annotation document = new Annotation(theSentence);
pipeline.annotate(document);
```

Since the pipeline can perform different types of processing, a list of CoreMap objects is used to access the words and tags. The Annotation class' get method returns the list of sentences, as shown here.

```
List<CoreMap> sentences =
    document.get(SentencesAnnotation.class);
```

The contents of the CoreMap objects can be accessed using its get method. The method's argument is the class for the information needed. As shown in the following code example, tokens are accessed using the TextAnnotation class, and the POS tags can be retrieved using the PartOfSpeechAnnotation class. Each word of each sentence and its tags is displayed:

```
for (CoreMap sentence : sentences) {
    for (CoreLabel token : sentence.get(TokensAnnotation.class)) {
        String word = token.get(TextAnnotation.class);
        String pos = token.get(PartOfSpeechAnnotation.class);
        System.out.print(word + "/" + pos + " ");
    }
    System.out.println();
}
```

The output will be as follows:

```
The/DT voyage/NN of/IN the/DT Abraham/NNP Lincoln/NNP was/VBD for/IN a/DT
long/JJ time/NN marked/VBN by/IN no/DT special/JJ incident/NN ./.
```

The pipeline can use additional options to control how the tagger works. For example, by default the `english-left3words-distsim.tagger` tagger model is used. We can specify a different model using the `pos.model` property, as shown here. There is also a `pos.maxlen` property to control the maximum sentence size:

```
props.put("pos.model",
    "C:/.../Models/english-caseless-left3words-distsim.tagger");
```

Sometimes it is useful to have a tagged document that is XML formatted. The `StanfordCoreNLP` class' `xmlPrint` method will write out such a document. The method's first argument is the annotator to be displayed. Its second argument is the `OutputStream` object to write to. In the following code sequence, the previous tagging results are written to standard output. It is enclosed in a try-catch block to handle IO exceptions:

```
try {
    pipeline.xmlPrint(document, System.out);
} catch (IOException ex) {
    // Handle exceptions
}
```

A partial listing of the results is as follows. Only the first two words and the last word are displayed. Each token tag contains the word, its position, and its POS tag:

```
<?xml version="1.0" encoding="UTF-8"?>
<?xml-stylesheet href="CoreNLP-to-HTML.xsl" type="text/xsl"?>
<root>
<document>
<sentences>
<sentence id="1">
<tokens>
<token id="1">
<word>The</word>
<CharacterOffsetBegin>0</CharacterOffsetBegin>
<CharacterOffsetEnd>3</CharacterOffsetEnd>
<POS>DT</POS>
</token>
```

```
<token id="2">
<word>voyage</word>
<CharacterOffsetBegin>4</CharacterOffsetBegin>
<CharacterOffsetEnd>10</CharacterOffsetEnd>
<POS>NN</POS>
</token>

        ...
<token id="17">
<word>.</word>
<CharacterOffsetBegin>83</CharacterOffsetBegin>
<CharacterOffsetEnd>84</CharacterOffsetEnd>
<POS>.</POS>
</token>
</tokens>
</sentence>
</sentences>
</document>
</root>
```

The `prettyPrint` method works in a similar manner:

```
pipeline.prettyPrint(document, System.out);
```

However, the output is not really that pretty, as shown here. The original sentence is displayed followed by each word, its position, and its tag. The output has been formatted to make it more readable:

```
The voyage of the Abraham Lincoln was for a long time marked by no
special incident.
[Text=The CharacterOffsetBegin=0 CharacterOffsetEnd=3 PartOfSpeech=DT]

[Text=voyage CharacterOffsetBegin=4 CharacterOffsetEnd=10
PartOfSpeech=NN]

[Text=of CharacterOffsetBegin=11 CharacterOffsetEnd=13 PartOfSpeech=IN]

[Text=the CharacterOffsetBegin=14 CharacterOffsetEnd=17 PartOfSpeech=DT]

[Text=Abraham CharacterOffsetBegin=18 CharacterOffsetEnd=25
PartOfSpeech=NNP]

  [Text=Lincoln CharacterOffsetBegin=26 CharacterOffsetEnd=33
PartOfSpeech=NNP]

  [Text=was CharacterOffsetBegin=34 CharacterOffsetEnd=37
PartOfSpeech=VBD]
```

```
[Text=for CharacterOffsetBegin=38 CharacterOffsetEnd=41 PartOfSpeech=IN]

[Text=a CharacterOffsetBegin=42 CharacterOffsetEnd=43 PartOfSpeech=DT]

[Text=long CharacterOffsetBegin=44 CharacterOffsetEnd=48
PartOfSpeech=JJ]

[Text=time CharacterOffsetBegin=49 CharacterOffsetEnd=53
PartOfSpeech=NN]

[Text=marked CharacterOffsetBegin=54 CharacterOffsetEnd=60
PartOfSpeech=VBN]

[Text=by CharacterOffsetBegin=61 CharacterOffsetEnd=63 PartOfSpeech=IN]

[Text=no CharacterOffsetBegin=64 CharacterOffsetEnd=66 PartOfSpeech=DT]

[Text=special CharacterOffsetBegin=67 CharacterOffsetEnd=74
PartOfSpeech=JJ]

[Text=incident CharacterOffsetBegin=75 CharacterOffsetEnd=83
PartOfSpeech=NN]

[Text=. CharacterOffsetBegin=83 CharacterOffsetEnd=84 PartOfSpeech=.]
```

Using LingPipe POS taggers

LingPipe uses the `Tagger` interface to support POS tagging. This interface has a single method: `tag`. It returns a `List` instance of the `Tagging` objects. These objects are the words and their tags. The interface is implemented by the `ChainCrf` and `HmmDecoder` classes.

The `ChainCrf` class uses linear-chain conditional random field decoding and estimation for determining tags. The `HmmDecoder` class uses an HMM to perform tagging. We will illustrate this class next.

The `HmmDecoder` class uses the `tag` method to determine the most likely (first best) tags. It also has a `tagNBest` method that scores the possible tagging and returns an iterator of these scored tagging. There are three POS models that come with the LingPipe, which can be downloaded from `http://alias-i.com/lingpipe/web/models.html`. These are listed in the following table. For our demonstration, we will use the Brown Corpus model:

Model	File
English General Text: Brown Corpus	`pos-en-general-brown.HiddenMarkovModel`
English Biomedical Text: MedPost Corpus	`pos-en-bio-medpost.HiddenMarkovModel`
English Biomedical Text: GENIA Corpus	`pos-en-bio-genia.HiddenMarkovModel`

Using the HmmDecoder class with Best_First tags

We start with a try-with-resources block to handle exceptions and the code to create the HmmDecoder instance, as shown next.

The model is read from the file and then used as the argument of the HmmDecoder constructor:

```
try (
        FileInputStream inputStream =
            new FileInputStream(getModelDir()
            + "//pos-en-general-brown.HiddenMarkovModel");
        ObjectInputStream objectStream =
            new ObjectInputStream(inputStream);) {
    HiddenMarkovModel hmm = (HiddenMarkovModel)
        objectStream.readObject();
    HmmDecoder decoder = new HmmDecoder(hmm);
    ...
} catch (IOException ex) {
  // Handle exceptions
} catch (ClassNotFoundException ex) {
  // Handle exceptions
};
```

We will perform tagging on theSentence variable. First, it needs to be tokenized. We will use an Indo-European tokenizer as shown here. The tokenizer method requires that the text string be converted to an array of chars. The tokenize method then returns an array of tokens as strings:

```
TokenizerFactory TOKENIZER_FACTORY =
    IndoEuropeanTokenizerFactory.INSTANCE;
char[] charArray = theSentence.toCharArray();
Tokenizer tokenizer =
    TOKENIZER_FACTORY.tokenizer(
        charArray, 0, charArray.length);
String[] tokens = tokenizer.tokenize();
```

The actual tagging is performed by the HmmDecoder class' tag method. However, this method requires a List instance of String tokens. This list is created using the Arrays class' asList method. The Tagging class holds a sequence of tokens and tags:

```
List<String> tokenList = Arrays.asList(tokens);
Tagging<String> tagString = decoder.tag(tokenList);
```

We are now ready to display the tokens and their tags. The following loop uses the `token` and `tag` methods to access the tokens and tags, respectively, in the `Tagging` object. They are then displayed:

```
for (int i = 0; i < tagString.size(); ++i) {
    System.out.print(tagString.token(i) + "/"
    + tagString.tag(i) + " ");
}
```

The output is as follows:

```
The/at voyage/nn of/in the/at Abraham/np Lincoln/np was/bedz for/in a/at
long/jj time/nn marked/vbn by/in no/at special/jj incident/nn ./.
```

Using the HmmDecoder class with NBest tags

The tagging process considers multiple combinations of tags. The `HmmDecoder` class' `tagNBest` method returns an iterator of the `ScoredTagging` objects that reflect the confidence of different orders. This method takes a token list and a number specifying the maximum number of results desired.

The previous sentence is not ambiguous enough to demonstrate the combination of tags. Instead, we will use the following sentence:

```
String[] sentence = {"Bill", "used", "the", "force",
    "to", "force", "the", "manager", "to",
    "tear", "the", "bill","in", "to."};
List<String> tokenList = Arrays.asList(sentence);
```

The example using this method is shown here starting with declarations for the number of results:

```
int maxResults = 5;
```

Using the decoder object created in the previous section, we apply the `tagNBest` method to it as follows:

```
Iterator<ScoredTagging<String>> iterator =
    decoder.tagNBest(tokenList, maxResults);
```

The iterator will allows us to access each of the five different scores. The `ScoredTagging` class possesses a `score` method that returns a value reflecting how well it believes it performs. In the following code sequence, a `printf` statement displays this score. This is followed by a loop where the token and its tag are displayed.

The result is a score followed by the word sequence with the tag attached:

```
while (iterator.hasNext()) {
    ScoredTagging<String> scoredTagging = iterator.next();
    System.out.printf("Score: %7.3f    Sequence: ",
        scoredTagging.score());
    for (int i = 0; i < tokenList.size(); ++i) {
        System.out.print(scoredTagging.token(i) + "/"
            + scoredTagging.tag(i) + " ");
    }
    System.out.println();
}
```

The output is as follows. Notice that the word "force" can have a tag of nn, jj, or vb:

```
Score: -148.796    Sequence: Bill/np used/vbd the/at force/nn to/to force/
vb the/at manager/nn to/to tear/vb the/at bill/nn in/in two./nn

Score: -154.434    Sequence: Bill/np used/vbn the/at force/nn to/to force/
vb the/at manager/nn to/to tear/vb the/at bill/nn in/in two./nn

Score: -154.781    Sequence: Bill/np used/vbd the/at force/nn to/in force/
nn the/at manager/nn to/to tear/vb the/at bill/nn in/in two./nn

Score: -157.126    Sequence: Bill/np used/vbd the/at force/nn to/to force/
vb the/at manager/jj to/to tear/vb the/at bill/nn in/in two./nn

Score: -157.340    Sequence: Bill/np used/vbd the/at force/jj to/to force/
vb the/at manager/nn to/to tear/vb the/at bill/nn in/in two./nn
```

Determining tag confidence with the HmmDecoder class

Statistical analysis can be performed using a lattice structure, which is useful for analyzing alternative word orderings. This structure represents forward/backward scores. The HmmDecoder class' tagMarginal method returns an instance of a TagLattice class, which represents a lattice.

We can examine each token of the lattice using an instance of the ConditionalClassification class. In the following example, the tagMarginal method returns a TagLattice instance. A loop is used to obtain the ConditionalClassification instance for each token in the lattice.

We are using the same `tokenList` instance developed in the previous section:

```
TagLattice<String> lattice = decoder.tagMarginal(tokenList);
for (int index = 0; index < tokenList.size(); index++) {
    ConditionalClassification classification =
        lattice.tokenClassification(index);

    ...
}
```

The `ConditionalClassification` class has a `score` and a `category` method. The `score` method returns a relative score for a given category. The `category` method returns this category, which is the tag. The token, its score, and category are displayed as shown here:

```
System.out.printf("%-8s",tokenList.get(index));
for (int i = 0; i < 4; ++i) {
    double score = classification.score(i);
    String tag = classification.category(i);
    System.out.printf("%7.3f/%-3s ",score,tag);
}
System.out.println();
```

The output is shown as follows:

```
Bill      0.974/np     0.018/nn     0.006/rb     0.001/nps
used      0.935/vbd    0.065/vbn    0.000/jj     0.000/rb
the       1.000/at     0.000/jj     0.000/pps    0.000/pp$$
force     0.977/nn     0.016/jj     0.006/vb     0.001/rb
to        0.944/to     0.055/in     0.000/rb     0.000/nn
force     0.945/vb     0.053/nn     0.002/rb     0.001/jj
the       1.000/at     0.000/jj     0.000/vb     0.000/nn
manager   0.982/nn     0.018/jj     0.000/nn$    0.000/vb
to        0.988/to     0.012/in     0.000/rb     0.000/nn
tear      0.991/vb     0.007/nn     0.001/rb     0.001/jj
the       1.000/at     0.000/jj     0.000/vb     0.000/nn
bill      0.994/nn     0.003/jj     0.002/rb     0.001/nns
in        0.990/in     0.004/rp     0.002/nn     0.001/jj
two.      0.960/nn     0.013/np     0.011/nns    0.008/rb
```

Training the OpenNLP POSModel

Training an OpenNLP POSModel is similar to the previous training examples.
A training file is needed and should be large enough to provide a good sample set.
Each sentence of the training file must be on a line by itself. Each line consists of a
token followed by the underscore character and then the tag.

The following training data was created using the first five sentences of *Chapter 5,
At A Venture* of *Twenty Thousands Leagues Under the Sea*. Although this is not a large
sample set, it is easy to create and adequate for illustration purposes.

It is saved in a file named sample.train:

```
The_DT voyage_NN of_IN the_DT Abraham_NNP Lincoln_NNP was_VBD for_IN a_DT
long_JJ time_NN marked_VBN by_IN no_DT special_JJ incident._NN
```

```
But_CC one_CD circumstance_NN happened_VBD which_WDT showed_VBD the_DT
wonderful_JJ dexterity_NN of_IN Ned_NNP Land,_NNP and_CC proved_VBD what_
WP confidence_NN we_PRP might_MD place_VB in_IN him._PRP$
```

```
The_DT 30th_JJ of_IN June,_NNP the_DT frigate_NN spoke_VBD some_DT
American_NNP whalers,_, from_IN whom_WP we_PRP learned_VBD that_IN they_
PRP knew_VBD nothing_NN about_IN the_DT narwhal._NN
```

```
But_CC one_CD of_IN them,_PRP$ the_DT captain_NN of_IN the_DT Monroe,_NNP
knowing_VBG that_IN Ned_NNP Land_NNP had_VBD shipped_VBN on_IN board_NN
the_DT Abraham_NNP Lincoln,_NNP begged_VBD for_IN his_PRP$ help_NN in_IN
chasing_VBG a_DT whale_NN they_PRP had_VBD in_IN sight._NN
```

We will demonstrate the creation of the model using the POSModel class' train
method and how the model can be saved to a file. We start with the declaration of
the POSModel instance variable:

```
POSModel model = null;
```

A try-with-resources block opens the sample file:

```
try (InputStream dataIn = new FileInputStream("sample.train");) {
   ...
} catch (IOException e) {
   // Handle excpetions
}
```

An instance of the `PlainTextByLineStream` class is created and used with the `WordTagSampleStream` class to create an `ObjectStream<POSSample>` instance. This puts the sample data into the format required by the `train` method:

```
ObjectStream<String> lineStream =
    new PlainTextByLineStream(dataIn, "UTF-8");
ObjectStream<POSSample> sampleStream =
    new WordTagSampleStream(lineStream);
```

The `train` method uses its parameters to specify the language, the sample stream, training parameters, and any dictionaries (none) needed, as shown here:

```
model = POSTaggerME.train("en", sampleStream,
    TrainingParameters.defaultParams(), null, null);
```

The output of this process is lengthy. The following output has been shortened to conserve space:

```
Indexing events using cutoff of 5

  Computing event counts...  done. 90 events
  Indexing...  done.
Sorting and merging events... done. Reduced 90 events to 82.
Done indexing.
Incorporating indexed data for training...
done.
  Number of Event Tokens: 82
      Number of Outcomes: 17
    Number of Predicates: 45
...done.
Computing model parameters ...
Performing 100 iterations.
  1:  ... loglikelihood=-254.98920096505964  0.1444444444444443
  2:  ... loglikelihood=-201.19283975630537  0.6
  3:  ... loglikelihood=-174.8849213436524  0.611111111111112
  4:  ... loglikelihood=-157.58164262220754  0.6333333333333333
  5:  ... loglikelihood=-144.69272379986646  0.6555555555555556
...
 99:  ... loglikelihood=-33.461128002846024  0.9333333333333333
100:  ... loglikelihood=-33.29073273669207  0.9333333333333333
```

To save the model to a file, we use the following code. The output stream is created and the POSModel class' serialize method saves the model to the en_pos_verne.bin file:

```
try (OutputStream modelOut = new BufferedOutputStream(
        new FileOutputStream(new File("en_pos_verne.bin")));) {
    model.serialize(modelOut);
} catch (IOException e) {
    // Handle exceptions
}
```

Summary

POS tagging is a powerful technique for identifying the grammatical parts of a sentence. It provides useful processing for downstream tasks such as question analysis and analyzing the sentiment of text. We will return to this subject when we address parsing in *Chapter 7, Using a Parser to Extract Relationships*.

Tagging is not an easy process due to the ambiguities found in most languages. The increasing use of textese only makes the process more difficult. Fortunately, there are models that can do a good job of identifying this type of text. However, as new terms and slang are introduced, these models need to be kept up to date.

We investigated the use of OpenNLP, the Stanford API, and LingPipe in support of tagging. These libraries used several different types of approaches to tag words including both rule-based and model-based approaches. We saw how dictionaries can be used to enhance the tagging process.

We briefly touched on the model training process. Pretagged sample texts are used as input to the process and a model emerges as output. Although we did not address validation of the model, this can be accomplished in a similar manner as accomplished in earlier chapters.

The various POS tagger approaches can be compared based on a number of factors such as their accuracy and how fast they run. Although we did not cover these issues here, there are numerous web resources available. One comparison that examines how fast they run can be found at http://mattwilkens.com/2008/11/08/evaluating-pos-taggers-speed/.

In the next chapter, we will examine techniques to classify documents based on their content.

6
Classifying Texts and Documents

In this chapter, we will demonstrate how to use various NLP APIs to perform text classification. This is not to be confused with text clustering. Clustering is concerned with the identification of text without the use of predefined categories. Classification, in contrast, uses predefined categories. We will focus on text classification where tags are assigned to text to specify its type.

The general approach used to perform text classification starts with the training of a model. The model is validated and then used to classify documents. We will focus on the training and usage steps.

Documents can be classified according to any number of attributes such as its subject, document type, time of publication, author, language used, and reading level. Some classification approaches require humans to label sample data.

Sentiment analysis is a type of classification. It is concerned with determining what text is trying to convey to a reader, usually in the form of a positive and negative attitude. We will investigate several techniques to perform this type of analysis.

How classification is used

Classifying text is used for a number of purposes:

- Spam detection
- Authorship attribution
- Sentiment analysis

- Age and gender identification
- Determining the subject of a document
- Language identification

Spamming is an unfortunate reality for most e-mail users. If an e-mail can be classified as spam, then it can be moved to a spam folder. A text message can be analyzed and certain attributes can be used to designate the e-mail as spam. These attributes can include misspellings, lack of an appropriate e-mail address for recipients, and a non-standard URL.

Classification has been used to determine the authorship of documents. This has been performed for historical documents such as for *The Federalist Papers* and for the book *Primary Colors* where the authors have been identified.

Sentiment analysis is a technique that determines the attitude of text. Movie reviews have been a popular domain but it can be used for almost any product review. This helps companies better assess how their product is perceived. Often, a negative or positive attribute is assigned to text. Sentiment analysis is also called opinion extraction/mining and subjectivity analysis. Consumer confidence and the performance of a stock market can be predicted from Twitter feeds and other sources.

Classification can be used to determine the age and gender of a text's author and to provide more insight into its author. Frequently, the number of pronouns, determiners, and noun phrases are used to identify the gender of a writer. Females tend to use more pronouns and males tend to use more determiners.

Determining the subject of text is useful when we need to organize a large number of documents. Search engines are very much concerned with this activity but it has also been used simply to place documents in different categories such as used with tag clouds. A tag cloud is a group of words reflecting the relative frequency of occurrence of each word.

The following image is an example of a tag cloud generated by IBM Word Cloud Generator (http://www.softpedia.com/get/Office-tools/Other-Office-Tools/IBM-Word-Cloud-Generator.shtml) and can be found at http://upload.wikimedia.org/wikipedia/commons/9/9e/Foundation-l_word_cloud_without_headers_and_quotes.png:

The identification of the language used by a document is supported using classification techniques. This analysis is useful for many NLP problems where we need to apply specific language models to the problem.

Understanding sentiment analysis

With sentiment analysis, we are concerned with who holds what type of feeling about a specific product or topic. This can tell us that citizens of a particular city hold positive or negative feelings about the performance of a sports team. They may hold a different sentiment about the team's performance versus its management.

It can be useful to automatically determine the sentiment for aspects, or attributes, of a product and then display the results in some meaningful manner. This is illustrated using a review of the 2014 Camry from Kelly Blue Book (`http://www.kbb.com/ toyota/camry/2014-toyota-camry/?r=471659652516861060`), as shown in the following figure.

The attributes, such as *Overall Rating* and *Value*, are depicted both as a bar graph and as a numeric value. The calculation of these values can be performed automatically using sentiment analysis.

Sentiment analysis can be applied to a sentence, a clause, or an entire document. Sentiment analysis may be either positive or negative or it could be a rating using numeric values such as 1 through 10. More complex attitude types are possible.

Further complicating the process, within a single sentence or document, different sentiments could be expressed against different topics.

How do we know which words have which types of sentiment? This question can be answered using sentiment lexicons. In this context, lexicons are dictionaries that contain the sentiment meanings of different words. The General Inquirer (http://www.wjh.harvard.edu/~inquirer/) is one such lexicon. It contains 1,915 words that are considered to be positive. It also contains a list for words denoting other attributes such as pain, pleasure, strong, and motivation. There are other lexicons such as the MPQA Subjectivity Cues Lexicon (http://mpqa.cs.pitt.edu/).

At times it may be desirable to build a lexicon. This is typically done using semi-supervised learning where a few labelled examples or rules are used to bootstrap the lexicon building process. This is useful when the domain of the lexicon being used does not match the domain of the problem area we are working on very well.

Not only are we interested in obtaining a positive or negative sentiment, we are interested in determining the attributes, sometimes called the target, of the sentiment. Consider the following example:

"The ride was very rough but the attendants did an excellent job of making us comfortable."

The sentence contains two sentiments: roughness and comfortable. The first was negative and the second was positive. The target, or attribute, of the positive sentiment was the job and the target of the negative sentiment was the ride.

Text classifying techniques

Classification is concerned with taking a specific document and determining if it fits into one of several other document groups. There are two basic techniques for classifying text:

- Rule-based
- Supervised Machine Learning

Rule-based classification uses a combination of words and other attributes organized around expert crafted rules. These can be very effective but creating them is a time-consuming process.

Supervised Machine Learning (SML) takes a collection of annotated training documents to create a model. The model is normally called the **classifier**. There are many different machine learning techniques including **Naive Bayes**, **Support-Vector Machine (SVM)**, and **k-nearest neighbor**.

We are not concerned with how these approaches work but the interested reader will find innumerable sources that expand upon these and other techniques.

Using APIs to classify text

We will use OpenNLP, Stanford API, and LingPipe to demonstrate various classification approaches. We will spend more time with LingPipe as it offers several different classification approaches.

Using OpenNLP

The DocumentCategorizer interface specifies methods to support the classification process. The interface is implemented by the DocumentCategorizerME class. This class will classify text into predefined categories using a maximum entropy framework. We will:

- Demonstrate how to train the model
- Illustrate how the model can be used

Training an OpenNLP classification model

First, we have to train our model because OpenNLP does not have prebuilt models. This process consists of creating a file of training data and then using the DocumentCategorizerME model to perform the actual training. The model created is typically saved in a file for later use.

The training file format consists of a series of lines where each line represents a document. The first word of the line is the category. The category is followed by text separated by whitespace. Here is an example for the dog category:

```
dog The most interesting feature of a dog is its ...
```

To demonstrate the training process, we created the en-animals.train file, where we created two categories: cats and dogs. For the training text, we used sections of Wikipedia. For dogs (http://en.wikipedia.org/wiki/Dog), we used the *As Pets* section. For cats (http://en.wikipedia.org/wiki/Cats_and_humans), we used the *Pet* section plus the first paragraph of the *Domesticated varieties* section. We also removed the numeric references from the sections.

The first part of each line is shown here:

```
dog The most widespread form of interspecies bonding occurs ...
dog There have been two major trends in the changing status of  ...
dog There are a vast range of commodity forms available to  ...
dog An Australian Cattle Dog in reindeer antlers sits on Santa's lap
...
dog A pet dog taking part in Christmas traditions ...
dog The majority of contemporary people with dogs describe their  ...
dog Another study of dogs' roles in families showed many dogs have
...
dog According to statistics published by the American Pet Products
...
```

```
dog The latest study using Magnetic resonance imaging (MRI) ...
cat Cats are common pets in Europe and North America, and their  ...
cat Although cat ownership has commonly been associated  ...
cat The concept of a cat breed appeared in Britain during ...
cat Cats come in a variety of colors and patterns. These are physical
...
cat A natural behavior in cats is to hook their front claws
periodically  ...
cat Although scratching can serve cats to keep their claws from
growing  ...
```

When creating training data, it is important to use a large enough sample size. The data we used is not sufficient for some analysis. However, as we will see, it does a pretty good job of identifying the categories correctly.

The DoccatModel class supports categorization and classification of text. A model is trained using the train method based on annotated text. The train method uses a string denoting the language and an ObjectStream<DocumentSample> instance holding the training data. The DocumentSample instance holds the annotated text and its category.

In the following example, the en-animal.train file is used to train the model. Its input stream is used to create a PlainTextByLineStream instance, which is then converted to an ObjectStream<DocumentSample> instance. The train method is then applied. The code is enclosed in a try-with-resources block to handle exceptions. We also created an output stream that we will use to persist the model:

```
DoccatModel model = null;
try (InputStream dataIn =
        new FileInputStream("en-animal.train");
     OutputStream dataOut =
        new FileOutputStream("en-animal.model");) {
    ObjectStream<String> lineStream
        = new PlainTextByLineStream(dataIn, "UTF-8");
    ObjectStream<DocumentSample> sampleStream =
        new DocumentSampleStream(lineStream);
    model = DocumentCategorizerME.train("en", sampleStream);
    ...
} catch (IOException e) {
// Handle exceptions
}
```

The output is as follows and has been shortened to conserve space:

```
Indexing events using cutoff of 5

  Computing event counts...  done. 12 events
  Indexing...  done.
Sorting and merging events... done. Reduced 12 events to 12.
Done indexing.
Incorporating indexed data for training...
done.
  Number of Event Tokens: 12
    Number of Outcomes: 2
  Number of Predicates: 30
...done.
Computing model parameters ...
Performing 100 iterations.
  1:  ... loglikelihood=-8.317766166719343  0.75
  2:  ... loglikelihood=-7.1439957443937265  0.75
  3:  ... loglikelihood=-6.560690872956419  0.75
  4:  ... loglikelihood=-6.106743124066829  0.75
  5:  ... loglikelihood=-5.721805583104927  0.8333333333333334
  6:  ... loglikelihood=-5.3891508904777785  0.8333333333333334
  7:  ... loglikelihood=-5.098768040466029  0.8333333333333334
...
 98:  ... loglikelihood=-1.4117372921765519  1.0
 99:  ... loglikelihood=-1.4052738190352423  1.0
100:  ... loglikelihood=-1.398916120150312  1.0
```

The model is saved as shown here using the `serialize` method. The model is saved to the `en-animal.model` file as opened in the previous try-with-resources block:

```
OutputStream modelOut = null;
modelOut = new BufferedOutputStream(dataOut);
model.serialize(modelOut);
```

Using DocumentCategorizerME to classify text

Once a model has been created, we can use the `DocumentCategorizerME` class to classify text. We need to read the model, create an instance of the `DocumentCategorizerME` class, and then invoke the `categorize` method to return an array of probabilities that will tell us which category the text best fits in.

Since we are reading from a file, exceptions need to be dealt with, as shown here:

```
try (InputStream modelIn =
        new FileInputStream(new File("en-animal.model"));) {
    ...
} catch (IOException ex) {
    // Handle exceptions
}
```

With the input stream, we create instances of the `DoccatModel` and `DocumentCategorizerME` classes as illustrated here:

```
DoccatModel model = new DoccatModel(modelIn);
DocumentCategorizerME categorizer =
    new DocumentCategorizerME(model);
```

The `categorize` method is called using a string as an argument. This returns an array of double values with each element containing the likelihood that the text belongs to a category. The `DocumentCategorizerME` class' `getNumberOfCategories` method returns the number of categories handled by the model. The `DocumentCategorizerME` class' `getCategory` method returns the category given an index.

We used these methods in the following code to display each category and its corresponding likelihood:

```
double[] outcomes = categorizer.categorize(inputText);
for (int i = 0; i<categorizer.getNumberOfCategories(); i++) {
    String category = categorizer.getCategory(i);
    System.out.println(category + " - " + outcomes[i]);
}
```

For testing, we used part of the Wikipedia article (`http://en.wikipedia.org/wiki/Toto_%28Oz%29`) for Toto, Dorothy's dog. We used the first sentence of *The classic books* section as declared here:

```
String toto = "Toto belongs to Dorothy Gale, the heroine of "
        + "the first and many subsequent books. In the first "
```

```
+ "book, he never spoke, although other animals, native "
+ "to Oz, did. In subsequent books, other animals "
+ "gained the ability to speak upon reaching Oz or "
+ "similar lands, but Toto remained speechless.";
```

To test for a cat, we used the first sentence of the Tortoiseshell and Calico section of the Wikipedia article (`http://en.wikipedia.org/wiki/Cats_and_humans`) as declared here:

```
String calico = "This cat is also known as a calimanco cat or "
              + "clouded tiger cat, and by the abbreviation 'tortie'. "
              + "In the cat fancy, a tortoiseshell cat is patched "
              + "over with red (or its dilute form, cream) and black "
              + "(or its dilute blue) mottled throughout the coat.";
```

Using the text for `toto`, we get the following output. This suggests that the text should be placed in the `dog` category:

dog - 0.5870711529777994

cat - 0.41292884702220056

Using `calico` instead yields these results:

dog - 0.28960436044424276

cat - 0.7103956395557574

We could have used the `getBestCategory` method to return only the best category. This method uses the array of outcomes and returns a string. The `getAllResults` method will return all of the results as a string. These two methods are illustrated here:

```
System.out.println(categorizer.getBestCategory(outcomes));
System.out.println(categorizer.getAllResults(outcomes));
```

The output will be as follows:

cat

dog [0.2896]   **cat** [0.7104]

Using Stanford API

The Stanford API supports several classifiers. We will examine the use of the `ColumnDataClassifier` class for general classification and the `StanfordCoreNLP` pipeline to perform sentiment analysis. The classifiers supported by the Stanford API can be difficult to use at times. With the `ColumnDataClassifier` class, we will demonstrate how to classify the size of boxes. With the pipeline, we will illustrate how to determine the positive or negative sentiment of short text phrases. The classifier can be downloaded from `http://www-nlp.stanford.edu/wiki/Software/Classifier`.

Using the ColumnDataClassifier class for classification

This classifier uses data with multiple values to describe the data. In this demonstration, we will use a training file to create a classifier. We will then use a test file to assess the performance of the classifier. The class uses a property file to configure the creation process.

We will be creating a classifier that attempts to classify a box based on its dimensions. Three categories will be possible: small, medium, and large. The height, width, and length dimensions of a box will be expressed as floating point numbers. They are used to characterize a box.

The properties file specifies parameter information and supplies data about the training and test files. There are many possible properties that can be specified. For this example, we will use only a few of the more relevant properties.

We will use the following properties file saved as `box.prop`. The first set of properties deal with the number of features that are contained in the training and test files. Since we used three values, three `realValued` columns are specified. The `trainFile` and `testFile` properties specify the location and names of the respective files:

```
useClassFeature=true
1.realValued=true
2.realValued=true
3.realValued=true
trainFile=.box.train
testFile=.box.test
```

The training and test files use the same format. Each line consists of a category followed by the defining values, each separated by a tab. The box.train training file consist of 60 entries and the box.test file consists of 30 entries. These files can be downloaded from www.packtpub.com. The first line of the box.train file follows here. The category is small; its height, width, and length are 2.34, 1.60, and 1.50, respectively:

```
small   2.34   1.60   1.50
```

The code to create the classifier is shown here. An instance of the ColumnDataClassifier class is created using the properties file as the constructor's argument. An instance of the Classifier interface is returned by the makeClassifier method. This interface supports three methods, two of which we will demonstrate. The readTrainingExamples method reads the training data from the training file:

```
ColumnDataClassifier cdc =
    new ColumnDataClassifier("box.prop");
Classifier<String, String> classifier =
    cdc.makeClassifier(cdc.readTrainingExamples("box.train"));
```

When executed, we get extensive output. We will discuss the more relevant parts here. The first part of the output repeats parts of the property file:

```
3.realValued = true
testFile = .box.test
...
trainFile = .box.train
```

The next part displays the number of datasets read along with various features' information, as shown here:

```
Reading dataset from box.train ... done [0.1s, 60 items].
numDatums: 60
numLabels: 3 [small, medium, large]
...
AVEIMPROVE      The average improvement / current value
EVALSCORE       The last available eval score
Iter ## evals ## <SCALING> [LINESEARCH] VALUE TIME |GNORM| {RELNORM}
AVEIMPROVE EVALSCORE
```

The classifier then iterates over the data to create the classifier:

```
Iter 1 evals 1 <D> [113M 3.107E-4] 5.985E1 0.00s |3.829E1| {1.959E-1}
0.000E0 -

Iter 2 evals 5 <D> [M 1.000E0] 5.949E1 0.01s |1.862E1| {9.525E-2} 3.058E-
3 -

Iter 3 evals 6 <D> [M 1.000E0] 5.923E1 0.01s |1.741E1| {8.904E-2} 3.485E-
3 -

. . .

Iter 21 evals 24 <D> [1M 2.850E-1] 3.306E1 0.02s |4.149E-1| {2.122E-3}
1.775E-4 -

Iter 22 evals 26 <D> [M 1.000E0] 3.306E1 0.02s

QNMinimizer terminated due to average improvement: | newest_val -
previous_val | / |newestVal| < TOL

Total time spent in optimization: 0.07s
```

At this point, the classifier is ready to use. Next, we use the test file to verify the classifier. We start by getting a line from the text file using the `ObjectBank` class' `getLineIterator` method. This class supports the conversion of data read into a more standardized form. The `getLineIterator` method returns one line at a time in a format that can be used by the classifier. The loop for this process is shown here:

```
for (String line :
        ObjectBank.getLineIterator("box.test", "utf-8")) {

    . . .

}
```

Within the for-each statement, a `Datum` instance is created from the line and then its `classOf` method is used to return the predicted category as shown here. The `Datum` interface supports objects that contain features. When used as the argument of the `classOf` method, the category determined by the classifier is returned:

```
Datum<String, String> datum = cdc.makeDatumFromLine(line);
System.out.println("Datum: {"
    + line + "]\tPredicted Category: "
    + classifier.classOf(datum));
```

When this sequence is executed, each line of the test file is processed and the predicted category is displayed, as follows. Only the first two and last two lines are shown here. The classifier was able to correctly classify all of the test data:

```
Datum: {small  1.33  3.50  5.43]  Predicted Category: medium
Datum: {small  1.18  1.73  3.14]  Predicted Category: small
```

```
...
Datum: {large   6.01   9.35   16.64]   Predicted Category: large
Datum: {large   6.76   9.66   15.44]   Predicted Category: large
```

To test an individual entry, we can use the makeDatumFromStrings method to create a Datum instance. In the next code sequence, a one-dimensional array of strings is created where each element represents data values for a box. The first entry, the category, is left null. The Datum instance is then used as the argument of the classOf method to predict its category:

```
String sample[] = {"", "6.90", "9.8", "15.69"};
Datum<String, String> datum =
    cdc.makeDatumFromStrings(sample);
System.out.println("Category: " + classifier.classOf(datum));
```

The output for this sequence is shown here, which correctly classifies the box:

```
Category: large
```

Using the Stanford pipeline to perform sentiment analysis

In this section, we will illustrate how the Stanford API can be used to perform sentiment analysis. We will use the StanfordCoreNLP pipeline to perform this analysis on different texts.

We will use three different texts as defined here. The review string is a movie review from Rotten Tomatoes (http://www.rottentomatoes.com/m/forrest_gump/) about the movie Forrest Gump:

```
String review = "An overly sentimental film with a somewhat "
    + "problematic message, but its sweetness and charm "
    + "are occasionally enough to approximate true depth "
    + "and grace. ";

String sam = "Sam was an odd sort of fellow. Not prone "
    + "to angry and not prone to merriment. Overall, "
    + "an odd fellow.";

String mary = "Mary thought that custard pie was the "
    + "best pie in the world. However, she loathed "
    + "chocolate pie.";
```

To perform this analysis, we need to use a sentiment annotator as shown here. This also requires the use of the tokenize, ssplit and parse annotators. The parse annotator provides more structural information about the text, which will be discussed in more detail in *Chapter 7, Using a Parser to Extract Relationships*:

```
Properties props = new Properties();
props.put("annotators", "tokenize, ssplit, parse, sentiment");
StanfordCoreNLP pipeline = new StanfordCoreNLP(props);
```

The text is used to create an Annotation instance, which is then used as the argument to the annotate method that performs the actual work, as shown here:

```
Annotation annotation = new Annotation(review);
pipeline.annotate(annotation);
```

The following array holds the strings for the different sentiments possible:

```
String[] sentimentText = {"Very Negative", "Negative",
    "Neutral", "Positive", "Very Positive"};
```

The Annotation class' get method returns an object that implements the CoreMap interface. In this case, these objects represent the results of splitting the input text into sentences, as shown in the following code. For each sentence, an instance of a Tree object is obtained that represents a tree structure containing a parse of the text for the sentiment. The getPredictedClass method returns an index into the sentimentText array reflecting the sentiment of the test:

```
for (CoreMap sentence : annotation.get(
        CoreAnnotations.SentencesAnnotation.class)) {
    Tree tree = sentence.get(
        SentimentCoreAnnotations.AnnotatedTree.class);
    int score = RNNCoreAnnotations.getPredictedClass(tree);
    System.out.println(sentimentText[score]);
}
```

When the code is executed using the review string, we get the following output:

```
Positive
```

The text, sam, consists of three sentences. The output for each is as follows, showing the sentiment for each sentence:

```
Neutral
Negative
Neutral
```

The text, `mary`, consists of two sentences. The output for each is as follows:

```
Positive
Neutral
```

Using LingPipe to classify text

We will use LingPipe to demonstrate a number of classification tasks including general text classification using trained models, sentiment analysis, and language identification. We will cover the following classification topics:

- Training text using the `Classified` class
- Training models using other training categories
- How to classify text using LingPipe
- Performing sentiment analysis using LingPipe
- Identifying the language used

Several of the tasks described in this section will use the following declarations. LingPipe comes with training data for several categories. The `categories` array contains the names of the categories packaged with LingPipe:

```
String[] categories = {"soc.religion.christian",
    "talk.religion.misc","alt.atheism","misc.forsale"};
```

The `DynamicLMClassifier` class is used to perform the actual classification. It is created using the `categories` array giving it the names of the categories to use. The `nGramSize` value specifies the number of contiguous items in a sequence used in the model for classification purposes:

```
int nGramSize = 6;
DynamicLMClassifier<NGramProcessLM> classifier =
    DynamicLMClassifier.createNGramProcess(
        categories, nGramSize);
```

Training text using the Classified class

General text classification using LingPipe involves training the `DynamicLMClassifier` class using training files and then using the class to perform the actual classification. LingPipe comes with several training datasets as found in the LingPipe directory, `demos/data/fourNewsGroups/4news-train`. We will use these to illustrate the training process. This example is a simplified version of the process found at `http://alias-i.com/lingpipe/demos/tutorial/classify/read-me.html`.

We start by declaring the training directory:

```
String directory = ".../demos";
File trainingDirectory = new File(directory
    + "/data/fourNewsGroups/4news-train");
```

In the training directory, there are four subdirectories whose names are listed in the `categories` array. In each subdirectory is a series of files with numeric names. These files contain newsgroups (http://qwone.com/~jason/20Newsgroups/) data that deal with that directories, names.

The process of training the model involves using each file and category with the `DynamicLMClassifier` class' `handle` method. The method will use the file to create a training instance for the category and then augment the model with this instance. The process uses nested for-loops.

The outer for-loop creates a `File` object using the directory's name and then applies the `list` method against it. The `list` method returns a list of the files in the directory. The names of these files are stored in the `trainingFiles` array, which will be used in the inner loop:

```
for (int i = 0; i < categories.length; ++i) {
    File classDir =
        new File(trainingDirectory, categories[i]);
    String[] trainingFiles = classDir.list();
    // Inner for-loop
}
```

The inner for-loop, as shown next, will open each file and read the text from the file. The `Classification` class represents a classification with a specified category. It is used with the text to create a `Classified` instance. The `DynamicLMClassifier` class' `handle` method updates the model with the new information:

```
for (int j = 0; j < trainingFiles.length; ++j) {
    try {
        File file = new File(classDir, trainingFiles[j]);
        String text = Files.readFromFile(file, "ISO-8859-1");
        Classification classification =
            new Classification(categories[i]);
        Classified<CharSequence> classified =
            new Classified<>(text, classification);
        classifier.handle(classified);
    } catch (IOException ex) {
        // Handle exceptions
    }
}
```

You can alternately use the `com.aliasi.util.Files` class instead in `java.io.File`, otherwise the `readFromFile` method will not be available.

The classifier can be serialized for later use as shown here. The `AbstractExternalizable` class is a utility class that supports the serialization of objects. It has a static `compileTo` method that accepts a `Compilable` instance and a `File` object. It writes the object to the file, as follows:

```
try {
    AbstractExternalizable.compileTo( (Compilable) classifier,
        new File("classifier.model"));
} catch (IOException ex) {
    // Handle exceptions
}
```

The loading of the classifier will be illustrated in the *Classifying text using LingPipe* section later in this chapter.

Using other training categories

Other newsgroups data can be found at `http://qwone.com/~jason/20Newsgroups/`. These collections of data can be used to train other models as listed in the following table. Although there are only 20 categories, they can be useful training models. Three different downloads are available where some have been sorted and in others, duplicate data has been removed:

Newsgroups	
comp.graphics	sci.crypt
comp.os.ms-windows.misc	sci.electronics
comp.sys.ibm.pc.hardware	sci.med
comp.sys.mac.hardware	sci.space
comp.windows.x	misc.forsale
rec.autos	talk.politics.misc
rec.motorcycles	talk.politics.guns
rec.sport.baseball	talk.politics.mideast
rec.sport.hockey	talk.religion.misc
alt.atheism	

Classifying text using LingPipe

To classify text, we will use the `DynamicLMClassifier` class' `classify` method. We will demonstrate its use with two different text sequences:

- `forSale`: The first is from `http://www.homes.com/for-sale/` where we use the first complete sentence

- `martinLuther`: The second is from `http://en.wikipedia.org/wiki/Martin_Luther` where we use the first sentence of the second paragraph

These strings are declared here:

```
String forSale =
    "Finding a home for sale has never been "
    + "easier. With Homes.com, you can search new "
    + "homes, foreclosures, multi-family homes, "
    + "as well as condos and townhouses for sale. "
    + "You can even search our real estate agent "
    + "directory to work with a professional "
    + "Realtor and find your perfect home.";
String martinLuther =
    "Luther taught that salvation and subsequently "
    + "eternity in heaven is not earned by good deeds "
    + "but is received only as a free gift of God's "
    + "grace through faith in Jesus Christ as redeemer "
    + "from sin and subsequently eternity in Hell.";
```

To reuse the classifier serialized in the previous section, use the `AbstractExternalizable` class' `readObject` method as shown here. We will use the `LMClassifier` class instead of the `DynamicLMClassifier` class. They both support the `classify` method but the `DynamicLMClassifier` class is not readily serializable:

```
LMClassifier classifier = null;
try {
    classifier = (LMClassifier)
        AbstractExternalizable.readObject(
            new File("classifier.model"));
} catch (IOException | ClassNotFoundException ex) {
    // Handle exceptions
}
```

In the next code sequence, we apply the `LMClassifier` class' `classify` method. This returns a `JointClassification` instance, which we use to determine the best match:

```
JointClassification classification =
    classifier.classify(text);
System.out.println("Text: " + text);
String bestCategory = classification.bestCategory();
System.out.println("Best Category: " + bestCategory);
```

For the `forSale` text, we get the following output:

```
Text: Finding a home for sale has never been easier. With Homes.com,
you can search new homes, foreclosures, multi-family homes, as well as
condos and townhouses for sale. You can even search our real estate agent
directory to work with a professional Realtor and find your perfect home.
```

```
Best Category: misc.forsale
```

For the `martinLuther` text, we get the following output:

```
Text: Luther taught that salvation and subsequently eternity in heaven
is not earned by good deeds but is received only as a free gift of God's
grace through faith in Jesus Christ as redeemer from sin and subsequently
eternity in Hell.
```

```
Best Category: soc.religion.christian
```

They both correctly classified the text.

Sentiment analysis using LingPipe

Sentiment analysis is performed in a very similar manner to that of general text classification. One difference is the use of only two categories: positive and negative.

We need to use data files to train our model. We will use a simplified version of the sentiment analysis performed at `http://alias-i.com/lingpipe/demos/tutorial/sentiment/read-me.html` using sentiment data found developed for movies (`http://www.cs.cornell.edu/people/pabo/movie-review-data/review_polarity.tar.gz`). This data was developed from 1,000 positive and 1,000 negative reviews of movies found in IMDb's movie archives.

These reviews need to be downloaded and extracted. A `txt_sentoken` directory will be extracted along with its two subdirectories: `neg` and `pos`. Both of these subdirectories contain movie reviews. Although some of these files can be held in reserve to evaluate the model created, we will use all of them to simplify the explanation.

We will start with re-initialization of variables declared in the *Using LingPipe to classify text* section. The `categories` array is set to a two-element array to hold the two categories. The `classifier` variable is assigned a new `DynamicLMClassifier` instance using the new category array and `nGramSize` of size 8:

```
categories = new String[2];
categories[0] = "neg";
categories[1] = "pos";
nGramSize = 8;
classifier = DynamicLMClassifier.createNGramProcess(
    categories, nGramSize);
```

As we did earlier, we will create a series of instances based on the contents found in the training files. We will not detail the following code as it is very similar to that found in the *Training text using the Classified class* section. The main difference is there are only two categories to process:

```
String directory = "...";
File trainingDirectory = new File(directory, "txt_sentoken");
for (int i = 0; i < categories.length; ++i) {
    Classification classification =
        new Classification(categories[i]);
    File file = new File(trainingDirectory, categories[i]);
    File[] trainingFiles = file.listFiles();
    for (int j = 0; j < trainingFiles.length; ++j) {
        try {
            String review = Files.readFromFile(
                trainingFiles[j], "ISO-8859-1");
            Classified<CharSequence> classified =
                new Classified<>(review, classification);
            classifier.handle(classified);
        } catch (IOException ex) {
            ex.printStackTrace();
        }
    }
}
```

The model is now ready to be used. We will use the review for the movie Forrest Gump:

```
String review = "An overly sentimental film with a somewhat "
    + "problematic message, but its sweetness and charm "
    + "are occasionally enough to approximate true depth "
    + "and grace. ";
```

We use the `classify` method to perform the actual work. It returns a `Classification` instance whose `bestCategory` method returns the best category, as shown here:

```
Classification classification = classifier.classify(review);
String bestCategory = classification.bestCategory();
System.out.println("Best Category: " + bestCategory);
```

When executed, we get the following output:

Best Category: pos

This approach will also work well for other categories of text.

Language identification using LingPipe

LingPipe comes with a model, `langid-leipzig.classifier`, trained for several languages and is found in the `demos/models` directory. A list of supported languages is found in the following table. This model was developed using training data derived from the Leipzig Corpora Collection (`http://corpora.uni-leipzig.de/`). Another good tool can be found at `http://code.google.com/p/language-detection/`.

Language	Abbreviation	Language	Abbreviation
Catalan	cat	Italian	it
Danish	dk	Japanese	jp
English	en	Korean	kr
Estonian	ee	Norwegian	no
Finnish	fi	Sorbian	sorb
French	fr	Swedish	se
German	de	Turkish	tr

To use this model, we use essentially the same code we used in the *Classifying text using LingPipe* section earlier in this chapter. We start with the same movie review of Forrest Gump:

```
String text = "An overly sentimental film with a somewhat "
    + "problematic message, but its sweetness and charm "
    + "are occasionally enough to approximate true depth "
    + "and grace. ";
System.out.println("Text: " + text);
```

The `LMClassifier` instance is created using the `langid-leipzig.classifier` file:

```
LMClassifier classifier = null;
try {
    classifier = (LMClassifier)
        AbstractExternalizable.readObject(
            new File(".../langid-leipzig.classifier"));
} catch (IOException | ClassNotFoundException ex) {
    // Handle exceptions
}
```

The `classify` method is used followed by the application of the `bestCategory` method to obtain the best language fit, as shown here:

```
Classification classification = classifier.classify(text);
String bestCategory = classification.bestCategory();
System.out.println("Best Language: " + bestCategory);
```

The output is as follows with English being chosen:

Text: An overly sentimental film with a somewhat problematic message, but its sweetness and charm are occasionally enough to approximate true depth and grace.

Best Language: en

The following code example uses the first sentence of the Swedish Wikipedia entry in Swedish (`http://sv.wikipedia.org/wiki/Svenska`) for the text:

```
text = "Svenska är ett östnordiskt språk som talas av cirka "
    + "tio miljoner personer[1], främst i Finland "
    + "och Sverige.";
```

The output, as shown here, correctly selects the Swedish language:

Text: Svenska är ett östnordiskt språk som talas av cirka tio miljoner personer[1], främst i Finland och Sverige.

Best Language: se

Training can be conducted in the same way as done for the previous LingPipe models. Another consideration when performing language identification is that the text may be written in multiple languages. This can complicate the language detection process.

Summary

In this chapter, we discussed the issues surrounding the classification of text and examined several approaches to perform this process. The classification of text is useful for many activities such as detecting e-mail spamming, determining who the author of a document may be, performing gender identification, and language identification.

We also demonstrated how sentiment analysis is performed. This analysis is concerned with determining whether a piece of text is positive or negative in nature. It is also possible to assess other sentiment attributes.

Most of the approaches we used required us to first create a model based on training data. Normally, this model needs to be validated using a set of test data. Once the model has been created, it is usually easy to use.

In the next chapter, we will investigate the parsing process and how it contributes to extracting relationships from text.

7
Using Parser to Extract Relationships

Parsing is the process of creating a parse tree for a textual unit. This unit may be for a line of code or a sentence. It is easy to do for computer languages, since they were designed to make the task easy. However, this has made it harder to write code. Natural language parsing is considerably more difficult. This is due to the ambiguity found in natural languages. This ambiguity makes a language difficult to learn but offers great flexibility and expressive power. Here, we are not interested in parsing computer languages, but rather natural languages.

A parse tree is a hierarchical data structure that represents the syntactic structure of a sentence. Often, this is presented as a tree graph with a root as we will illustrate shortly. We will use the parse tree to help identify relationships between entities in the tree.

Parsing is used for many tasks, including:

- Machine translation of languages
- Synthesizing speech from text
- Speech recognition
- Grammar checking
- Information extraction

Coreference resolution is the condition where two or more expressions in text refer to the same individual or thing. For example, in this sentence:

"Ted went to the party where he made an utter fool of himself."

The words "Ted", "he", and "himself" refer to the same entity, "Ted". This is important in determining the correct interpretation of text and in determining the relative importance of text sections. We will demonstrate how the Stanford API addresses this problem.

Extracting relationships and information from text is an important NLP task. Relationships may exist between entities, such as the subject of a sentence and either its object, other entities, or perhaps its behavior. We may also want to identify relationships and present them in a structured form. We can use this information either to present the results for immediate use by people or to format the relationships so that they can be better utilized for a downstream task.

In this chapter, we will examine the parsing process and see how the parse tree is used. We will examine the relationship extraction process and investigate relationship types, use extracted relationships, and learn to use NLP APIs.

Relationship types

There are many possible relationship types. A few categories and examples of relationships are found in the following table. An interesting site that contains a multitude of relationships is Freebase (https://www.freebase.com/). It is a database of people, places, and things organized by categories. The WordNet thesaurus (http://wordnet.princeton.edu/) contains a number of relationships.

Relationship	Example
Personal	father-of, sister-of, girlfriend-of
Organizational	subsidiary-of, subcommittee–of
Spatial	near-to, northeast-of, under
Physical	part-of, composed-of
Interactions	bonds-with, associates-with, reacts-with

Name Entity Recognition is a low level type of NLP classification that was covered in *Chapter 4, Finding People and Things*. However, many applications need to go beyond this and identify different types of relationships. For example, when NER is applied to identify individuals, then knowing that we are dealing with a person can further refine the relationships present.

Once these entities have been identified, then links can be created to their containing documents or used as indexes. For question answering applications, named entities are often used for answers. When a sentiment of text is determined, it needs to be attributed to some entity.

For example, consider the following input:

```
He was the last person to see Fred.
```

Using OpenNLP NER as input with the preceding sentence, as we did in *Chapter 4*, *Finding People and Things*, we get the following output:

```
Span: [7..9) person
Entity: Fred
```

Using the OpenNLP parser, we get a lot more information about the sentence:

```
(TOP (S (NP (PRP He)) (VP (VBD was) (NP (NP (DT the) (JJ last) (NN
person)) (SBAR (S (VP (TO to) (VP (VB see)))))))) (. Fred.)))
```

Consider the following input:

```
The cow jumped over the moon.
```

For the preceding sentence, the parser returns this:

```
(TOP (S (NP (DT The) (NN cow)) (VP (VBD jumped) (PP (IN over) (NP (DT
the) (NN moon))))))
```

There are two types of parsing:

- **Dependency**: This focuses on the relationship between words
- **Phrase structure**: This deals with phrases and their recursive structure

Dependencies can use labels such as subject, determiner, and prepositions to find relationships. Parsing techniques include shift-reduce, spanning tree, and cascaded chunking. We are not concerned about these differences here, but will focus on the use and outcome of various parsers.

Understanding parse trees

Parse trees represent hierarchical relationships between elements of text. For example, a dependency tree shows the relationship between the grammatical elements of a sentence. Let's reconsider the following sentence:

```
The cow jumped over the moon.
```

A parse tree for the sentence is shown here. It was generated using the techniques found in *Using the LexicalizedParser class* later in this chapter:

```
(ROOT
  (S
    (NP (DT The) (NN cow))
```

```
(VP (VBD jumped)
  (PP (IN over)
    (NP (DT the) (NN moon)))))
(. .)))
```

The sentence can be graphically depicted as shown in the following figure. It was generated using the application found at `http://nlpviz.bpodgursky.com/home`. Another editor that allows you to examine text in a graphical manner is GrammarScope (`http://grammarscope.sourceforge.net/`). This is a Stanford supported tool that uses a Swing-based GUI to generate a parse tree, a grammatical structure, typed dependencies, and a semantic graph of text.

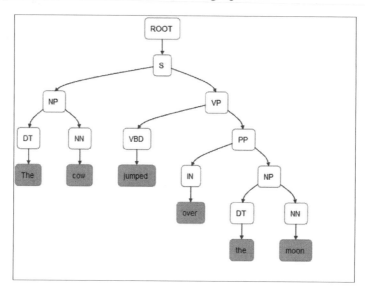

However, there may be more than one way of parsing a sentence. Parsing is difficult because it is necessary to handle a wide range of text where many ambiguities may exist. The following output illustrates other possible dependency trees for the previous example sentence. The tree was generated using OpenNLP, as will be demonstrated in the *Using OpenNLP* section later in the chapter:

```
(TOP (S (NP (DT The) (NN cow)) (VP (VBD jumped) (PP (IN over) (NP (DT
the) (NN moon))))))
(TOP (S (NP (DT The) (NN cow)) (VP (VP (VBD jumped) (PRT (RP over))) (NP
(DT the) (NN moon)))))
(TOP (S (NP (DT The) (NNS cow)) (VP (VBD jumped) (PP (IN over) (NP (DT
the) (NN moon))))))
```

Each of these represents a slightly different parse of the same sentence. The most likely parse is shown first.

Using extracted relationships

Relationships extracted can be used for a number of purposes including:

- Building knowledge bases
- Creating directories
- Product searches
- Patent analysis
- Stock analysis
- Intelligence analysis

An example of how relationships can be presented is illustrated by Wikipedia's Infobox, as shown in the following figure. This Infobox is for the entry Oklahoma and contains relationships types such as official language, capital, and details about its area.

There are many databases built using Wikipedia that extract relationships and information such as:

- **Resource Description Framework (RDF)**: This uses triples such as Yosemite-location-California, where the location is the relation. This can be found at `http://www.w3.org/RDF/`.

- **DBPedia**: This holds over one billion triples and is an example of a knowledge base created from Wikipedia. This can be found at `http://dbpedia.org/About`.

Another simple, but interesting example, is the Infobox that is presented when a Google search of "planet mercury" is made. As shown in the following screenshot, not only do we get a list of links for the query but we also see a list of relations and images for Mercury displayed on the right-hand side of the page:

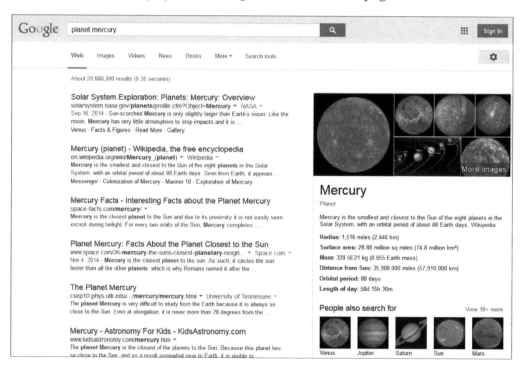

Information extraction is also used to create Web indexes. These indexes are developed for a site to allow a user to navigate through the site. An example of a web index for the U.S. Census Bureau (`http://www.census.gov/main/www/a2z`) is shown in the following screenshot:

Extracting relationships

There are a number of techniques available to extract relationships. These can be grouped as follows:

- Hand-built patterns
- Supervised methods
- Semi-supervised or unsupervised methods
    - Bootstrapping methods
    - Distant supervision methods
    - Unsupervised methods

Hand-built models are used when we have no training data. This can occur with new business domains or entirely new types of projects. These often require the use of rules. A rule might be:

"If the word "actor" or "actress" is used and not the word "movie" or "commercial", then the text should be classified as a play."

However, this approach takes a lot of effort and needs to be adjusted for the actual text in-hand.

If only a little training data is amiable, then the Naive Bayes classifier is a good choice. When more data is available, then techniques such as SVM, Regularized Logistic Regression, and Random forest can be used.

Although it is useful to understand these techniques in more detail, we will not cover them here as our focus is on the use of these techniques.

Using NLP APIs

We will use the OpenNLP and Stanford APIs to demonstrate parsing and the extraction of relation information. LingPipe can also be used but will not be discussed here. An example of how LingPipe is used to parse biomedical literature can be found at http://alias-i.com/lingpipe-3.9.3/demos/tutorial/medline/read-me.html.

Using OpenNLP

Parsing text is simple using the ParserTool class. Its static parseLine method accepts three arguments and returns a Parser instance. These arguments are:

- A string containing the text to be parsed
- A Parser instance
- An integer specifying how many parses are to be returned

The Parser instance holds the elements of the parse. The parses are returned in order of their probability. To create a Parser instance, we will use the ParserFactory class' create method. This method uses a ParserModel instance that we will create using the en-parser-chunking.bin file.

This process is shown here, where an input stream for the model file is created using a try-with-resources block. The ParserModel instance is created followed by a Parser instance:

```
String fileLocation = getModelDir() +
    "/en-parser-chunking.bin";
try (InputStream modelInputStream =
            new FileInputStream(fileLocation);) {
    ParserModel model = new ParserModel(modelInputStream);
    Parser parser = ParserFactory.create(model);
    ...
```

```
} catch (IOException ex) {
    // Handle exceptions
}
```

We will use a simple sentence to demonstrate the parsing process. In the following code sequence, the `parseLine` method is invoked using a value of 3 for the third argument. This will return the top three parses:

```
String sentence = "The cow jumped over the moon";
Parse parses[] = ParserTool.parseLine(sentence, parser, 3);
```

Next, the parses are displayed along with their probabilities, as shown here:

```
for(Parse parse : parses) {
    parse.show();
    System.out.println("Probability: " + parse.getProb());
}
```

The output is as follows:

```
(TOP (S (NP (DT The) (NN cow)) (VP (VBD jumped) (PP (IN over) (NP (DT
the) (NN moon))))))
```

Probability: -1.043506016751117

```
(TOP (S (NP (DT The) (NN cow)) (VP (VP (VBD jumped) (PRT (RP over))) (NP
(DT the) (NN moon)))))
```

Probability: -4.248553665013661

```
(TOP (S (NP (DT The) (NNS cow)) (VP (VBD jumped) (PP (IN over) (NP (DT
the) (NN moon))))))
```

Probability: -4.761071294573854

Notice that each parse produces a slightly different order and assignment of tags. The following output shows the first parse formatted to make it easier to read:

```
(TOP
    (S
        (NP
            (DT The)
            (NN cow)
        )
        (VP
            (VBD jumped)
            (PP
                (IN over)
                (NP
```

```
                                    (DT the)
                                    (NN moon)
                             )
                     )
                 )
             )
         )
```

The showCodeTree method can be used instead to display parent-child relationships:

```
    parse.showCodeTree();
```

The output for the first parse is shown here. The first part of each line shows the element levels enclosed in brackets. The tag is displayed next followed by two hash values separated by ->. The first number is for the element and the second number is its parent. For example, in the third line, it shows the proper noun, The, to have a parent of the noun phrase, The cow:

```
[0]  S -929208263 -> -929208263 TOP The cow jumped over the moon

[0.0] NP -929237012 -> -929208263 S The cow

[0.0.0] DT -929242488 -> -929237012 NP The

[0.0.0.0] TK -929242488 -> -929242488 DT The

[0.0.1] NN -929034400 -> -929237012 NP cow

[0.0.1.0] TK -929034400 -> -929034400 NN cow

[0.1] VP -928803039 -> -929208263 S jumped over the moon

[0.1.0] VBD -928822205 -> -928803039 VP jumped

[0.1.0.0] TK -928822205 -> -928822205 VBD jumped

[0.1.1] PP -928448468 -> -928803039 VP over the moon

[0.1.1.0] IN -928460789 -> -928448468 PP over

[0.1.1.0.0] TK -928460789 -> -928460789 IN over

[0.1.1.1] NP -928195203 -> -928448468 PP the moon

[0.1.1.1.0] DT -928202048 -> -928195203 NP the

[0.1.1.1.0.0] TK -928202048 -> -928202048 DT the

[0.1.1.1.1] NN -927992591 -> -928195203 NP moon

[0.1.1.1.1.0] TK -927992591 -> -927992591 NN moon
```

Another way of accessing the elements of the parse is through the `getChildren` method. This method returns an array of the `Parse` objects each representing an element of the parse. Using various `Parse` methods, we can get each element's text, tag, and labels. This is illustrated here:

```
Parse children[] = parse.getChildren();
for (Parse parseElement : children) {
    System.out.println(parseElement.getText());
    System.out.println(parseElement.getType());
    Parse tags[] = parseElement.getTagNodes();
    System.out.println("Tags");
    for (Parse tag : tags) {
        System.out.println("[" + tag + "]"
            + " type: " + tag.getType()
            + "  Probability: " + tag.getProb()
            + "  Label: " + tag.getLabel());
    }
}
```

The output of this sequence is as follows:

```
The cow jumped over the moon

S

Tags
[The] type: DT  Probability: 0.9380626549164167  Label: null
[cow] type: NN  Probability: 0.9574993337971017  Label: null
[jumped] type: VBD  Probability: 0.9652983971550483  Label: S-VP
[over] type: IN  Probability: 0.7990638213315913  Label: S-PP
[the] type: DT  Probability: 0.9848023215770413  Label: null
[moon] type: NN  Probability: 0.9942338356992393  Label: null
```

Using the Stanford API

There are several approaches to parsing available in the Stanford NLP API. First, we will demonstrate a general purposes parser, the `LexicalizedParser` class. Then, we will illustrate how the result of the parser can be displayed using the `TreePrint` class. This will be followed by a demonstration of how to determine word dependencies using the `GrammaticalStructure` class.

Using the LexicalizedParser class

The LexicalizedParser class is a lexicalized PCFG parser. It can use various models to perform the parsing process. The apply method is used with a List instance of the CoreLabel objects to create a parse tree.

In the following code sequence, the parser is instantiated using the englishPCFG. ser.gz model:

```
String parserModel = ".../models/lexparser/englishPCFG.ser.gz";
LexicalizedParser lexicalizedParser =
    LexicalizedParser.loadModel(parserModel);
```

The list instance of the CoreLabel objects is created using the Sentence class' toCoreLabelList method. The CoreLabel objects contain a word and other information. There are no tags or labels for these words. The words in the array have been effectively tokenized.

```
String[] senetenceArray = {"The", "cow", "jumped", "over",
    "the", "moon", "."};
List<CoreLabel> words =
    Sentence.toCoreLabelList(senetenceArray);
```

The apply method can now be invoked:

```
Tree parseTree = lexicalizedParser.apply(words);
```

One simple approach to display the result of the parse is to use the pennPrint method, which displays the parse tree in the same way as the Penn TreeBank does (http://www.sfs.uni-tuebingen.de/~dm/07/autumn/795.10/ptb-annotation-guide/root.html):

```
parseTree.pennPrint();
```

The output is as follows:

```
(ROOT
  (S
    (NP (DT The) (NN cow))
    (VP (VBD jumped)
      (PP (IN over)
        (NP (DT the) (NN moon))))
    (. .)))
```

The Tree class provides numerous methods for working with parse trees.

Using the TreePrint class

The `TreePrint` class provides a simple way to display the tree. An instance of the class is created using a string describing the display format to be used. An array of valid output formats can be obtained using the static `outputTreeFormats` variable and are listed in the following table:

Tree Format Strings		
penn	dependencies	collocations
oneline	typedDependencies	semanticGraph
rootSymbolOnly	typedDependenciesCollapsed	conllStyleDependencies
words	latexTree	conll2007
wordsAndTags	xmlTree	

Stanford uses type dependencies to describe the grammatical relationships that exist within a sentence. These are detailed in the Stanford Typed Dependencies Manual (`http://nlp.stanford.edu/software/dependencies_manual.pdf`).

The following code example illustrates how the `TreePrint` class can be used. The `printTree` method performs the actual display operation.

In this case, the `TreePrint` object is created showing the type dependencies "collapsed".

```
TreePrint treePrint =
    new TreePrint("typedDependenciesCollapsed");
treePrint.printTree(parseTree);
```

The output of this sequence is as follows where the number reflects its position within the sentence:

```
det(cow-2, The-1)
nsubj(jumped-3, cow-2)
root(ROOT-0, jumped-3)
det(moon-6, the-5)
prep_over(jumped-3, moon-6)
```

Using the "penn" string to create the object results in the following output:

```
(ROOT
  (S
    (NP (DT The) (NN cow))
    (VP (VBD jumped)
      (PP (IN over)
        (NP (DT the) (NN moon))))
    (. .)))
```

The "dependencies" string produces a simple list of dependencies:

```
dep(cow-2,The-1)
dep(jumped-3,cow-2)
dep(null-0,jumped-3,root)
dep(jumped-3,over-4)
dep(moon-6,the-5)
dep(over-4,moon-6)
```

The formats can be combined using commas. The following example will result in both the penn style and the typedDependenciesCollapsed formats being used for the display:

```
"penn,typedDependenciesCollapsed"
```

Finding word dependencies using the GrammaticalStructure class

Another approach to parse text is to use the LexicalizedParser object created in the previous section in conjunction with the TreebankLanguagePack interface. A **Treebank** is a text corpus that has been annotated with syntactic or semantic information, providing information about a sentence's structure. The first major Treebank was the Penn TreeBank (http://www.cis.upenn.edu/~treebank/). Treebanks can be created manually or semiautomatically.

The next example illustrates how a simple string can be formatted using the parser. A tokenizer factory creates a tokenizer.

The `CoreLabel` class that we discussed in the *Using the LexicalizedParser class* section is used here:

```
String sentence = "The cow jumped over the moon.";
TokenizerFactory<CoreLabel> tokenizerFactory =
    PTBTokenizer.factory(new CoreLabelTokenFactory(), "");
Tokenizer<CoreLabel> tokenizer =
    tokenizerFactory.getTokenizer(new StringReader(sentence));
List<CoreLabel> wordList = tokenizer.tokenize();
parseTree = lexicalizedParser.apply(wordList);
```

The `TreebankLanguagePack` interface specifies methods for working with a Treebank. In the following code, a series of objects are created that culminate with the creation of a `TypedDependency` instance, which is used to obtain dependency information about elements of a sentence. An instance of a `GrammaticalStructureFactory` object is created and used to create an instance of a `GrammaticalStructure` class.

As this class' name implies, it stores grammatical information between elements in the tree:

```
TreebankLanguagePack tlp =
    lexicalizedParser.treebankLanguagePack;
GrammaticalStructureFactory gsf =
    tlp.grammaticalStructureFactory();
GrammaticalStructure gs =
    gsf.newGrammaticalStructure(parseTree);
List<TypedDependency> tdl = gs.typedDependenciesCCprocessed();
```

We can simply display the list as shown here:

```
System.out.println(tdl);
```

The output is as follows:

```
[det(cow-2, The-1), nsubj(jumped-3, cow-2), root(ROOT-0, jumped-3),
det(moon-6, the-5), prep_over(jumped-3, moon-6)]
```

This information can also be extracted using the `gov`, `reln`, and `dep` methods, which return the governor word, the relationship, and the dependent element, respectively, as illustrated here:

```
for(TypedDependency dependency : tdl) {
    System.out.println("Governor Word: [" + dependency.gov()
        + "] Relation: [" + dependency.reln().getLongName()
        + "] Dependent Word: [" + dependency.dep() + "]");
}
```

The output is as follows:

```
Governor Word: [cow/NN] Relation: [determiner] Dependent Word: [The/DT]

Governor Word: [jumped/VBD] Relation: [nominal subject] Dependent Word:
[cow/NN]

Governor Word: [ROOT] Relation: [root] Dependent Word: [jumped/VBD]

Governor Word: [moon/NN] Relation: [determiner] Dependent Word: [the/DT]

Governor Word: [jumped/VBD] Relation: [prep_collapsed] Dependent Word:
[moon/NN]
```

From this, we can gleam the relationships within a sentence and the elements of the relationship.

Finding coreference resolution entities

Coreference resolution refers to the occurrence of two or more expressions in text that refer to the same person or entity. Consider the following sentence:

"He took his cash and she took her change and together they bought their lunch."

There are several coreferences in this sentence. The word "his" refers to "He" and the word "her" refers to "she". In addition, "they" refers to both "He" and "she".

An **endophora** is a coreference of an expression that either precedes it or follows it. Endophora can be classified as anaphors or cataphors. In the following sentence, the word "It", is the anaphor that refers to its antecedent, "the earthquake":

"Mary felt the earthquake. It shook the entire building."

In the next sentence, "she" is a cataphor as it points to the postcedent, "Mary":

"As she sat there, Mary felt the earthquake."

The Stanford API supports coreference resolution with the `StanfordCoreNLP` class using a `dcoref` annotation. We will demonstrate the use of this class with the previous sentence.

We start with the creation of the pipeline and the use of the `annotate` method, as shown here:

```
String sentence = "He took his cash and she took her change "
    + "and together they bought their lunch.";
Properties props = new Properties();
props.put("annotators",
```

```
            "tokenize, ssplit, pos, lemma, ner, parse, dcoref");
    StanfordCoreNLP pipeline = new StanfordCoreNLP(props);
    Annotation annotation = new Annotation(sentence);
    pipeline.annotate(annotation);
```

The `Annotation` class' `get` method, when used with an argument of
`CorefChainAnnotation.class`, will return a `Map` instance of the `CorefChain`
objects, as shown here. These objects contain information about the coreferences
found in the sentence:

```
    Map<Integer, CorefChain> corefChainMap =
        annotation.get(CorefChainAnnotation.class);
```

The set of the `CorefChain` objects is indexed using integers. We can iterate over
these objects as shown here. The key set is obtained and then each `CorefChain`
object is displayed:

```
    Set<Integer> set = corefChainMap.keySet();
    Iterator<Integer> setIterator = set.iterator();
    while(setIterator.hasNext()) {
        CorefChain corefChain =
            corefChainMap.get(setIterator.next());
        System.out.println("CorefChain: " + corefChain);
    }
```

The following output is generated:

CorefChain: CHAIN1-["He" in sentence 1, "his" in sentence 1]

CorefChain: CHAIN2-["his cash" in sentence 1]

CorefChain: CHAIN4-["she" in sentence 1, "her" in sentence 1]

CorefChain: CHAIN5-["her change" in sentence 1]

CorefChain: CHAIN7-["they" in sentence 1, "their" in sentence 1]

CorefChain: CHAIN8-["their lunch" in sentence 1]

We get more detailed information using methods of the `CorefChain` and
`CorefMention` classes. The latter class contains information about a specific
coreference found in the sentence.

Add the following code sequence to the body of the previous while loop to obtain
and display this information. The `startIndex` and `endIndex` fields of the class refer
to the position of the words in the sentence:

```
    System.out.print("ClusterId: " + corefChain.getChainID());
    CorefMention mention = corefChain.getRepresentativeMention();
```

```
System.out.println(" CorefMention: " + mention
    + " Span: [" + mention.mentionSpan + "]");

List<CorefMention> mentionList =
    corefChain.getMentionsInTextualOrder();
Iterator<CorefMention> mentionIterator =
    mentionList.iterator();
while(mentionIterator.hasNext()) {
    CorefMention cfm = mentionIterator.next();
    System.out.println("\tMention: " + cfm
        + " Span: [" + mention.mentionSpan + "]");
    System.out.print("\tMention Mention Type: "
        + cfm.mentionType + " Gender: " + cfm.gender);
    System.out.println(" Start: " + cfm.startIndex
        + " End: " + cfm.endIndex);
}
System.out.println();
```

The output is as follows. Only the first and last mentions are displayed to conserve space:

CorefChain: CHAIN1-["He" in sentence 1, "his" in sentence 1]

ClusterId: 1 CorefMention: "He" in sentence 1 Span: [He]

  Mention: "He" in sentence 1 Span: [He]

  Mention Type: PRONOMINAL Gender: MALE Start: 1 End: 2

  Mention: "his" in sentence 1 Span: [He]

  Mention Type: PRONOMINAL Gender: MALE Start: 3 End: 4

...

CorefChain: CHAIN8-["their lunch" in sentence 1]

ClusterId: 8 CorefMention: "their lunch" in sentence 1 Span: [their lunch]

  Mention: "their lunch" in sentence 1 Span: [their lunch]

  Mention Type: NOMINAL Gender: UNKNOWN Start: 14 End: 16

Extracting relationships for a question-answer system

In this section, we will examine an approach for extracting relationships that can be useful for answering queries. Possible/candidate queries include:

- `Who is/was the 14th president of the United States?`
- `What is the 1st president's home town?`
- `When was Herbert Hoover president?`

The process of answering these types of questions is not easy. We will demonstrate one approach to answer certain types of questions, but we will simplify many aspects of the process. Even with these restrictions, we will find that the system responds well to the queries.

This process consists of several steps:

1. Finding word dependencies
2. Identifying the type of questions
3. Extracting its relevant components
4. Searching the answer
5. Presenting the answer

We will show the general framework to identify whether a question is of the types who, what, when, or where. Next, we will investigate some of the issues required to answer the "who" type questions.

To keep the example simple, we will restrict the questions to those relating to presidents of the U.S.. A simple database of presidential facts will be used to look up the answer to a question.

Finding the word dependencies

The question is stored as a simple string:

```
String question =
    "Who is the 32nd president of the United States?";
```

We will use the `LexicalizedParser` class as developed in the *Finding word dependencies using the GrammaticalStructure class* section. The relevant code is duplicated here for your convenience:

```
String parserModel = ".../englishPCFG.ser.gz";
LexicalizedParser lexicalizedParser =
    LexicalizedParser.loadModel(parserModel);

TokenizerFactory<CoreLabel> tokenizerFactory =
    PTBTokenizer.factory(new CoreLabelTokenFactory(), "");
Tokenizer<CoreLabel> tokenizer =
    tokenizerFactory.getTokenizer(new StringReader(question));
List<CoreLabel> wordList = tokenizer.tokenize();
Tree parseTree = lexicalizedParser.apply(wordList);

TreebankLanguagePack tlp =
    lexicalizedParser.treebankLanguagePack();
GrammaticalStructureFactory gsf =
    tlp.grammaticalStructureFactory();
GrammaticalStructure gs =
    gsf.newGrammaticalStructure(parseTree);
List<TypedDependency> tdl = gs.typedDependenciesCCprocessed();
System.out.println(tdl);
for (TypedDependency dependency : tdl) {
    System.out.println("Governor Word: [" + dependency.gov()
        + "] Relation: [" + dependency.reln().getLongName()
        + "] Dependent Word: [" + dependency.dep() + "]");
}
```

When executed with the question, we get the following output:

```
[root(ROOT-0, Who-1), cop(Who-1, is-2), det(president-5, the-3),
amod(president-5, 32nd-4), nsubj(Who-1, president-5), det(States-9, the-
7), nn(States-9, United-8), prep_of(president-5, States-9)]

Governor Word: [ROOT] Relation: [root] Dependent Word: [Who/WP]

Governor Word: [Who/WP] Relation: [copula] Dependent Word: [is/VBZ]

Governor Word: [president/NN] Relation: [determiner] Dependent Word:
[the/DT]

Governor Word: [president/NN] Relation: [adjectival modifier] Dependent
Word: [32nd/JJ]

Governor Word: [Who/WP] Relation: [nominal subject] Dependent Word:
[president/NN]
```

Governor Word: [States/NNPS] Relation: [determiner] Dependent Word: [the/DT]

Governor Word: [States/NNPS] Relation: [nn modifier] Dependent Word: [United/NNP]

Governor Word: [president/NN] Relation: [prep_collapsed] Dependent Word: [States/NNPS]

This information provides the foundation to determine the type of question.

Determining the question type

The relationships detected suggest ways to detect different types of questions. For example, to determine whether it is a "who" type question, we can check whether the relationship is nominal subject and the governor is who.

In the following code, we iterate over the question type dependencies to determine whether it matches this combination, and if so, call the processWhoQuestion method to process the question:

```
for (TypedDependency dependency : tdl) {
    if ("nominal subject".equals( dependency.reln().getLongName())
        && "who".equalsIgnoreCase( dependency.gov().originalText())) {
        processWhoQuestion(tdl);
    }
}
```

This simple distinction worked reasonably well. It will correctly identify all of the following variations to the same question:

Who is the 32nd president of the United States?

Who was the 32nd president of the United States?

The 32nd president of the United States was who?

The 32nd president is who of the United States?

We can also determine other question types using different selection criteria. The following questions typify other question types:

What was the 3rd President's party?

When was the 12th president inaugurated?

Where is the 30th president's home town?

We can determine the question type using the relations as suggested in the following table:

Question type	Relation	Governor	Dependent
What	nominal subject	what	NA
When	adverbial modifier	NA	when
Where	adverbial modifier	NA	where

This approach does require hardcoding the relationships.

Searching for the answer

Once we know the type of question, we can use the relations found in the text to answer the question. To illustrate this process, we will develop the `processWhoQuestion` method. This method uses the `TypedDependency` list to garner the information needed to answer a "who" type question about presidents. Specifically, we need to know which president they are interested in, based on the president's ordinal rank.

We will also need a list of presidents to search for relevant information. The `createPresidentList` method was developed to perform this task. It reads a file, `PresidentList`, containing the president's name, inauguration year, and last year in office. The file uses the following format and can be downloaded from `www.packtpub.com`:

George Washington   (1789-1797)

The following `createPresidentList` method demonstrates the use of OpenNLP's `SimpleTokenizer` class to tokenize each line. A variable number of tokens make up a president's name. Once that is determined, the dates are easily extracted:

```
public List<President> createPresidentList() {
    ArrayList<President> list = new ArrayList<>();
    String line = null;
    try (FileReader reader = new FileReader("PresidentList");
            BufferedReader br = new BufferedReader(reader)) {
        while ((line = br.readLine()) != null) {
            SimpleTokenizer simpleTokenizer =
                SimpleTokenizer.INSTANCE;
```

```
            String tokens[] = simpleTokenizer.tokenize(line);
            String name = "";
            String start = "";
            String end = "";
            int i = 0;
            while (!"(".equals(tokens[i])) {
                name += tokens[i] + " ";
                i++;
            }
            start = tokens[i + 1];
            end = tokens[i + 3];
            if (end.equalsIgnoreCase("present")) {
                end = start;
            }
            list.add(new President(name,
                Integer.parseInt(start),
                Integer.parseInt(end)));
        }
    } catch (IOException ex) {
        // Handle exceptions
    }
    return list;
}
```

A President class holds presidential information, as shown here. The getter methods have been left out:

```
public class President {
    private String name;
    private int start;
    private int end;

    public President(String name, int start, int end) {
        this.name = name;
        this.start = start;
        this.end = end;
    }
    ...
}
```

The `processWhoQuestion` method follows. We use type dependencies again to extract the ordinal value of the question. If the governor is `president` and the `adjectival modifier` is the relation, then the dependent word is the ordinal. This string is passed to the `getOrder` method, which returns the ordinal as an integer. We add 1 to it since the list of presidents also started at one:

```
public void processWhoQuestion(List<TypedDependency> tdl) {
    List<President> list = createPresidentList();
    for (TypedDependency dependency : tdl) {
        if ("president".equalsIgnoreCase(
                dependency.gov().originalText())
                && "adjectival modifier".equals(
                    dependency.reln().getLongName())) {
            String positionText =
                dependency.dep().originalText();
            int position = getOrder(positionText)-1;
            System.out.println("The president is "
                + list.get(position).getName());
        }
    }
}
```

The `getOrder` method is as follows and simply takes the first numeric characters and converts them to an integer. A more sophisticated version would look at other variations including words such as "first" and "sixteenth":

```
private static int getOrder(String position) {
    String tmp = "";
    int i = 0;
    while (Character.isDigit(position.charAt(i))) {
        tmp += position.charAt(i++);
    }
    return Integer.parseInt(tmp);
}
```

When executed, we get the following output:

The president is Franklin D . Roosevelt

This implementation is a simple example of how information can be extracted from a sentence and used to answer questions. The other types of questions can be implemented in a similar fashion and are left as an exercise for the reader.

Summary

We have discussed the parsing process and how it can be used to extract relationships from text. It can be used for a number of purposes including grammar checking and machine translation of text. There are numerous text relations possible. These include such relationships as father of, near to, and under. They are concerned with how elements of text are related to each other.

Parsing the text will return relationships that exist within the text. These relationships can be used to extract information of interest. We demonstrated a number of techniques using the OpenNLP and Stanford APIs to parse text.

We also explained how the Stanford API can be used to find coreference resolutions within text. This occurs when two or more expressions, such as "he" or "they", refer to the same person.

We concluded with an example of how a parser is used to extract relations from a sentence. These relations were used to extract information to answer simple "who" type queries about U.S. presidents.

In the next chapter, we will investigate how the techniques developed in this and the previous chapters can be used to solve more complicated problems.

8
Combined Approaches

In this chapter, we will address several issues surrounding the use of combinations of techniques to solve NLP problems. We start with a brief introduction to the process of preparing data. This is followed by a discussion on pipelines and their construction. A pipeline is nothing more than a sequence of tasks integrated to solve some problems. The chief advantage of a pipeline is the ability to insert and remove various elements of the pipeline to solve a problem in a slightly different manner.

The Stanford API supports a good pipeline architecture, which we have used repeatedly in this book. We will expand upon the details of this approach and then show how OpenNLP can be used to construct a pipeline.

Preparing data for processing is an important first step in solving many NLP problems. We introduced the data preparation process in *Chapter 1, Introduction to NLP,* and then discussed the normalization process in *Chapter 2, Finding Parts of Text.* In this chapter, we will focus on extracting text from different data sources, such as HTML, Word, and PDF documents, to be precise.

The Stanford `StanfordCoreNLP` class is a good example of a pipeline that is easily used. In a sense, it is preconstructed. The actual tasks performed are dependent on the annotations added. This works well for many types of problems.

However, other NLP APIs do not support pipeline architecture as directly as Stanford APIs; while more difficult to construct, these approaches can be more flexible for many applications. We demonstrate this construction process using OpenNLP.

Preparing data

Text extraction is an early step in most NLP tasks. Here, we will quickly cover how text extraction can be performed for HTML, Word, and PDF documents. Although there are several APIs that support these tasks, we will use:

- Boilerpipe (`https://code.google.com/p/boilerpipe/`) for HTML
- POI (`http://poi.apache.org/index.html`) for Word
- PDFBox (`http://pdfbox.apache.org/`) for PDF

Some APIs support the use of XML for input and output. For example, the Stanford `XMLUtils` class provides support for reading XML files and manipulating XML data. The LingPipe's `XMLParser` class will parse XML text.

Organizations store their data in many forms and frequently it is not in simple text files. Presentations are stored in PowerPoint slides, specifications are created using Word documents, and companies provide marketing and other materials in PDF documents. Most organizations have an Internet presence, which means that much useful information is found in HTML documents. Due to the widespread nature of these data sources, we need to use tools to extract their text for processing.

Using Boilerpipe to extract text from HTML

There are several libraries available for extracting text from HTML documents. We will demonstrate how to use Boilerpipe (`https://code.google.com/p/boilerpipe/`) to perform this operation. This is a flexible API that not only extracts the entire text of an HTML document but can also extract selected parts of an HTML document such as its title and individual text blocks.

We will use the HTML page at `http://en.wikipedia.org/wiki/Berlin` to illustrate the use of Boilerpipe. Part of this page is shown in the following screenshot. In order to use Boilerpipe, you will need to download the binary for the Xerces Parser found at `http://xerces.apache.org/index.html`.

We start by creating a URL object that represents this page as shown here. The try-catch block handles exceptions:

```
try {
    URL url = new
    URL("http://en.wikipedia.org/wiki/Berlin");
    ...
    } catch (MalformedURLException ex) {
       // Handle exceptions
    } catch (BoilerpipeProcessingException | SAXException
          | IOException ex) {
       // Handle exceptions
}
```

We will use two classes to extract text. The first is the HTMLDocument class that represents the HTML document. The second is the TextDocument class that represents the text within an HTML document. It consists of one or more TextBlock objects that can be accessed individually if needed.

In the following sequence, a HTMLDocument instance is created for the Berlin page. The BoilerpipeSAXInput class uses this input source to create a TextDocument instance. It then uses the TextDocument class' getText method to retrieve the text. This method uses two arguments. The first argument specifies whether to include the TextBlock instances marked as content. The second argument specifies whether noncontent TextBlock instances should be included. In this example, both types of TextBlock instances are included:

```
HTMLDocument htmlDoc = HTMLFetcher.fetch(url);
InputSource is = htmlDoc.toInputSource();
TextDocument document =
    new BoilerpipeSAXInput(is).getTextDocument();
System.out.println(document.getText(true, true));
```

The output of this sequence is quite large since the page is large. A partial listing of the output is as follows:

```
Berlin

From Wikipedia, the free encyclopedia

Jump to: navigation , search

This article is about the capital of Germany.  For other uses, see Berlin
(disambiguation) .

...

Privacy policy

About Wikipedia

Disclaimers

Contact Wikipedia

Developers

Mobile view
```

The getTextBlocks method will return a list of TextBlock objects for the document. Various methods allow you to access the text and information about the text such as the number of words in a block.

Using POI to extract text from Word documents

The Apache POI Project (`http://poi.apache.org/index.html`) is an API used to extract information from Microsoft Office products. It is an extensive library that allows information extraction from Word documents and other office products, such as Excel and Outlook.

When downloading the API for POI, you will also need to use XMLBeans (`http://xmlbeans.apache.org/`), which supports POI. The binaries for XMLBeans can be downloaded from `http://www.java2s.com/Code/Jar/x/Downloadxmlbeans230jar.htm`.

Our interest is in demonstrating how to use POI to extract text from Word documents. To demonstrate this use, we will use a file called `TestDocument.docx`, as shown in the following screenshot:

There are several different file formats used by different versions of Word. To simplify the selection of which text extraction class to use, we will use the ExtractorFactory factory class.

Although the POI's capabilities are considerable, the process of extracting text is simple. As shown here, a FileInputStream object representing the file, TestDocument.docx, is used by the ExtractorFactory class' createExtractor method to select the appropriate POITextExtractor instance. This is the base class for several different extractors. The getText method is applied to the extractor to get the text:

```
try {
    FileInputStream fis =
        new FileInputStream("TestDocument.docx");
    POITextExtractor textExtractor =
        ExtractorFactory.createExtractor(fis);
    System.out.println(textExtractor.getText());
} catch (IOException ex) {
    // Handle exceptions
} catch (OpenXML4JException | XmlException ex) {
    // Handle exceptions
}
```

A part of the output is as follows:

`Pirates`

`Pirates are people who use ships to rob other ships. At least this is a common definition. They have also been known as buccaneers, corsairs, and privateers. In`

`...`

`Our list includes:`

`Gan Ning`

`Awilda`

`...`

`Get caught`

`Walk the plank`

`This is not a recommended occupation.`

It can be useful to know more about a Word document. POI supports a `POIXMLPropertiesTextExtractor` class that gives us access to core, extended, and custom properties of a document. There are two ways of readily getting a string containing many of these properties.

- The first approach uses the `getMetadataTextExtractor` method and then the `getText` method, as shown here:

```
POITextExtractor metaExtractor =
    textExtractor.getMetadataTextExtractor();
System.out.println(metaExtractor.getText());
```

- The second approach creates an instance of the `POIXMLPropertiesTextExtractor` class using `XWPFDocument` representing the Word document, as illustrated here:

```
fis = new FileInputStream("TestDocument.docx");
POIXMLPropertiesTextExtractor properties =
    new POIXMLPropertiesTextExtractor(new
    XWPFDocument(fis));
System.out.println(properties.getText());
```

The output of either approach is shown here:

```
Created = Sat Jan 03 18:27:00 CST 2015
CreatedString = 2015-01-04T00:27:00Z
Creator = Richard
LastModifiedBy = Richard
LastPrinted = Sat Jan 03 18:27:00 CST 2015
LastPrintedString = 2015-01-04T00:27:00Z
Modified = Mon Jan 05 14:01:00 CST 2015
ModifiedString = 2015-01-05T20:01:00Z
Revision = 3
Application = Microsoft Office Word
AppVersion = 12.0000
Characters = 762
CharactersWithSpaces = 894
Company =
HyperlinksChanged = false
Lines = 6
```

```
LinksUpToDate = false
Pages = 1
Paragraphs = 1
Template = Normal.dotm
TotalTime = 20
```

There is a CoreProperties class that holds a core set of properties for the document. The getCoreProperties method provides access to these properties:

```
CoreProperties coreProperties = properties.getCoreProperties();
System.out.println(properties.getCorePropertiesText());
```

These properties are listed here:

```
Created = Sat Jan 03 18:27:00 CST 2015
CreatedString = 2015-01-04T00:27:00Z
Creator = Richard
LastModifiedBy = Richard
LastPrinted = Sat Jan 03 18:27:00 CST 2015
LastPrintedString = 2015-01-04T00:27:00Z
Modified = Mon Jan 05 14:01:00 CST 2015
ModifiedString = 2015-01-05T20:01:00Z
Revision = 3
```

There are individual methods with access to specific properties such as the getCreator, getCreated, and getModified methods. Extended properties, represented by the ExtendedProperties class, are available through the getExtendedProperties method, as shown here:

```
ExtendedProperties extendedProperties =
    properties.getExtendedProperties();
System.out.println(properties.getExtendedPropertiesText());
```

The output is as follows:

```
Application = Microsoft Office Word
AppVersion = 12.0000
Characters = 762
CharactersWithSpaces = 894
Company =
```

```
HyperlinksChanged = false

Lines = 6

LinksUpToDate = false

Pages = 1

Paragraphs = 1

Template = Normal.dotm

TotalTime = 20
```

Methods such as getApplication, getAppVersion, and getPages give access to specific extended properties.

Using PDFBox to extract text from PDF documents

The Apache PDFBox (http://pdfbox.apache.org/) project is an API for processing PDF documents. It supports the extraction of text and other tasks such as document merging, form filling, and PDF creation. We will only illustrate the text extraction process.

To demonstrate the use of POI, we will use a file called TestDocument.pdf. This file was saved as a PDF document using the TestDocument.docx file as shown in the *Using POI to extract text from Word documents* section.

The process is straightforward. A File object is created for the PDF document. The PDDocument class represents the document and the PDFTextStripper class performs the actual text extraction using the getText method, as shown here:

```java
try {
    File file = new File("TestDocument.pdf");
    PDDocument pdDocument = PDDocument.load(file);
    PDFTextStripper stripper = new PDFTextStripper();
    String text = stripper.getText(pdDocument);
    System.out.println(text);
    pdDocument.close();
} catch (IOException ex) {
    // Handle exceptions
}
```

Due to its length, only part of the output is shown here:

```
Pirates

Pirates are people who use ships to rob other ships. At least this is a
common definition. They have also been known as buccaneers, corsairs, and
privateers. In

...

Our list includes:

⊠ Gan Ning

⊠ Awilda

...

4. Get caught

5. Walk the plank

This is not a recommended occupation.
```

The extraction includes special characters for the bullets and numbers for the numbered sequences.

Pipelines

A **pipeline** is nothing more than a sequence of operations where the output of one operation is used as the input to another operation. We have seen it used in several examples in previous chapters but they have been relatively short. In particular, we saw how the Stanford StanfordCoreNLP class, with its use of annotators objects, supports the concept of pipelines nicely. We will discuss this approach in the next section.

One of the advantages of a pipeline, if structured properly, is that it allows the easy addition and removal of processing elements. For example, if one step of the pipeline converts token to lowercase, then it can be easy to simply remove this step with the remaining elements of the pipeline left untouched.

However, some pipelines are not always this flexible. One step may require a previous step in order to work properly. In a pipeline, such as the one supported by the StanfordCoreNLP class, the following set of annotators is needed to support POS processing:

```
props.put("annotators", "tokenize, ssplit, pos");
```

If we leave out the `ssplit` annotator, the following exception is generated:

```
java.lang.IllegalArgumentException: annotator "pos" requires
annotator "ssplit"
```

Although the Stanford pipeline does not require a lot of effort to set up, other pipelines may. We will demonstrate the latter approach in the *Creating a pipeline to search text* section.

Using the Stanford pipeline

In this section, we will discuss the Stanford pipeline in more detail. Although we have used it in several examples in this book, we have not fully explored its capabilities. Having used this pipeline before, you are now in a better position to understand how it can be used. Upon reading this section, you will be able to better assess its capabilities and applicability to your needs.

The `edu.stanford.nlp.pipeline` package holds the `StanfordCoreNLP` and `annotator` classes. The general approach uses the following code sequence where the `text` string is processed. The `Properties` class holds the annotation names as shown here:

```
String text = "The robber took the cash and ran.";
Properties props = new Properties();
props.put("annotators",
    "tokenize, ssplit, pos, lemma, ner, parse, dcoref");
StanfordCoreNLP pipeline = new StanfordCoreNLP(props);
```

The `Annotation` class represents the text to be processed. The constructor, used in the next code segment, takes the string and adds a `CoreAnnotations.TextAnnotation` instance to the `Annotation` object. The `StanfordCoreNLP` class' `annotate` method will apply the annotations specified in the property list to the `Annotation` object:

```
Annotation annotation = new Annotation(text);
pipeline.annotate(annotation);
```

`CoreMap` interface is the base interface for all annotable objects. It uses class objects for keys. The `TextAnnotation` annotation type is a `CoreMap` key for the text. A `CoreMap` key is intended to be used with various types of annotations such as those defined in the properties list. The value depends on the key type.

The hierarchy of classes and interfaces is depicted in the following diagram. It is a simplified version of the relationship between classes and interfaces as they relate to the the pipeline. The horizontal lines represent interface implementations and the vertical lines represent inheritance between classes.

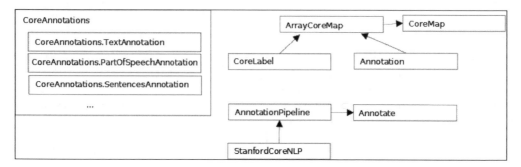

To verify the effect of the `annotate` method, we will use the following code sequence. The `keyset` method returns a set of all of the annotation keys currently held by the `Annotation` object. These keys are displayed before and after the `annotate` method is applied:

```
System.out.println("Before annotate method executed ");
Set<Class<?>> annotationSet = annotation.keySet();
for(Class c : annotationSet) {
    System.out.println("\tClass: " + c.getName());
}

pipeline.annotate(annotation);

System.out.println("After annotate method executed ");
annotationSet = annotation.keySet();
for(Class c : annotationSet) {
    System.out.println("\tClass: " + c.getName());
}
```

The following output shows that the creation of the `Annotation` object resulted in the `TextAnnotation` extension being added to the annotation. After the `annotate` method is executed, several additional annotations have been applied:

```
Before annotate method executed
  Class: edu.stanford.nlp.ling.CoreAnnotations.TextAnnotation
```

```
After annotate method executed
   Class: edu.stanford.nlp.ling.CoreAnnotations.TextAnnotation
   Class: edu.stanford.nlp.ling.CoreAnnotations.TokensAnnotation
   Class: edu.stanford.nlp.ling.CoreAnnotations.SentencesAnnotation
   Class: edu.stanford.nlp.dcoref.CorefCoreAnnotations.
CorefChainAnnotation
```

The CoreLabel class implements the CoreMap interface. It represents a single word with annotation information attached to it. The information attached depends on the properties set when the pipeline is created. However, there will always be positional information available such as its beginning and ending position or the whitespace before and after the entity.

The get method for either CoreMap or CoreLabel returns information specific to its argument. The get method is overloaded and returns a value dependent on the type of its argument. For example, here is the declaration of the SentencesAnnotation class. It implements CoreAnnotation<List<CoreMap>>:

```
public static class CoreAnnotations.SentencesAnnotation
    extends Object
    implements CoreAnnotation<List<CoreMap>>
```

When used in the following statement, the SentencesAnnotation class returns a List<CoreMap> instance:

```
List<CoreMap> sentences =
    annotation.get(SentencesAnnotation.class);
```

In a similar manner, the TokensAnnotation class implements CoreAnnotation<List<CoreLabel>> as shown here:

```
public static class CoreAnnotations.TokensAnnotation
    extends Object
    implements CoreAnnotation<List<CoreLabel>>
```

Its get method returns a list of CoreLabel objects that are used within a for-each statement:

```
for (CoreLabel token : sentence.get(TokensAnnotation.class)) {
```

In previous chapters, we have used the SentencesAnnotation class to access the sentences in an annotation, as shown here:

```
List<CoreMap> sentences =
    annotation.get(SentencesAnnotation.class);
```

The `CoreLabel` class has been used to access individual words in a sentence as demonstrated here:

```
for (CoreMap sentence : sentences) {
    for (CoreLabel token:
            sentence.get(TokensAnnotation.class)) {
        String word = token.get(TextAnnotation.class);
        String pos = token.get(PartOfSpeechAnnotation.class);
    }
}
```

Annotator options can be found at `http://nlp.stanford.edu/software/corenlp.shtml`. The following code example illustrates how to use an annotator to specify the POS model. The `pos.model` property is set to the model desired using the `Property` class' `put` method:

```
props.put("pos.model",
    "C:/.../Models/english-caseless-left3words-distsim.tagger");
```

A summary of the annotators is found in the following table. The first column is the string used in the properties' list. The second column lists only the basic annotation class, and the third column specifies how it is typically used:

Property name	Basic annotation class	Usage
tokenize	`TokensAnnotation`	Tokenization
cleanxml	`XmlContextAnnotation`	Remove XML tokens
ssplit	`SentencesAnnotation`	Splits tokens into sentences
pos	`PartOfSpeechAnnotation`	Creates POS tags
lemma	`LemmaAnnotation`	Generates lemmas
ner	`NamedEntityTagAnnotation`	Creates NER tags
regexner	`NamedEntityTagAnnotation`	Creates NER tags based on regular expressions
sentiment	`SentimentCoreAnnotations`	Sentiment analysis
truecase	`TrueCaseAnnotation`	True case analysis
parse	`TreeAnnotation`	Generates a parse tree
depparse	`BasicDependenciesAnnotation`	Syntactic dependency parser
dcoref	`CorefChainAnnotation`	Performs coreference resolution
relation	`MachineReadingAnnotations`	Relation extractor

Consider the following sequence to create a pipeline:

```
String text = "The robber took the cash and ran.";
Properties props = new Properties();
props.put("annotators",
    "tokenize, ssplit, pos, lemma, ner, parse, dcoref");
StanfordCoreNLP pipeline = new StanfordCoreNLP(props);
```

We get the following output for the annotation process. We can see each annotator as it is applied:

`Adding annotator tokenize`

`TokenizerAnnotator: No tokenizer type provided. Defaulting to PTBTokenizer.`

`Adding annotator ssplit`

`edu.stanford.nlp.pipeline.AnnotatorImplementations:`

`Adding annotator pos`

`Reading POS tagger model from edu/stanford/nlp/models/pos-tagger/english-left3words/english-left3words-distsim.tagger ... done [2.5 sec].`

`Adding annotator lemma`

`Adding annotator ner`

`Loading classifier from edu/stanford/nlp/models/ner/english.all.3class.distsim.crf.ser.gz ... done [6.7 sec].`

`Loading classifier from edu/stanford/nlp/models/ner/english.muc.7class.distsim.crf.ser.gz ... done [5.0 sec].`

`Loading classifier from edu/stanford/nlp/models/ner/english.conll.4class.distsim.crf.ser.gz ... done [5.5 sec].`

`Adding annotator parse`

`Loading parser from serialized file edu/stanford/nlp/models/lexparser/englishPCFG.ser.gz ...done [0.9 sec].`

`Adding annotator dcoref`

When the `annotate` method is applied, we can use the `timingInformation` method to see how long each step of the process took, as shown here:

```
System.out.println("Total time: " + pipeline.timingInformation());
```

The output of the previous pipeline is as follows:

```
Total time: Annotation pipeline timing information:
TokenizerAnnotator: 0.0 sec.
WordsToSentencesAnnotator: 0.0 sec.
POSTaggerAnnotator: 0.0 sec.
MorphaAnnotator: 0.1 sec.
NERCombinerAnnotator: 0.0 sec.
ParserAnnotator: 2.5 sec.
DeterministicCorefAnnotator: 0.1 sec.
TOTAL: 2.8 sec. for 8 tokens at 2.9 tokens/sec.
```

Using multiple cores with the Stanford pipeline

The `annotate` method can also take advantage of multiple cores. It is an overloaded method where one version uses an instance of an `Iterable<Annotation>` as its parameter. It will process each `Annotation` instance using the processors available.

We will use the previously defined `pipeline` object to demonstrate this version of the `annotate` method.

First, we create four `Annotation` objects based on four short sentences, as shown here. To take full advantage of the technique, it would be better to use a larger set of data:

```
Annotation annotation1 = new Annotation(
    "The robber took the cash and ran.");
Annotation annotation2 = new Annotation(
    "The policeman chased him down the street.");
Annotation annotation3 = new Annotation(
    "A passerby, watching the action, tripped the thief "
    + "as he passed by.");
Annotation annotation4 = new Annotation(
    "They all lived happily ever after, except for the thief "
    + "of course.");
```

The `ArrayList` class implements the `Iterable` interface. We create an instance of this class and then add the four `Annotation` objects to it. The list is then assigned to an `Iterable` variable:

```
ArrayList<Annotation> list = new ArrayList();
list.add(annotation1);
list.add(annotation2);
list.add(annotation3);
list.add(annotation4);
Iterable<Annotation> iterable = list;
```

The `annotate` method is then executed:

```
pipeline.annotate(iterable);
```

We will use `annotation2` to show the results by displaying the word and it's POS, as shown here:

```
List<CoreMap> sentences =
    annotation2.get(SentencesAnnotation.class);

for (CoreMap sentence : sentences) {
    for (CoreLabel token :
            sentence.get(TokensAnnotation.class)) {
        String word = token.get(TextAnnotation.class);
        String pos = token.get(PartOfSpeechAnnotation.class);
        System.out.println("Word: " + word + " POS Tag: " + pos);
    }
}
```

The output is as follows:

```
Word: The POS Tag: DT
Word: policeman POS Tag: NN
Word: chased POS Tag: VBD
Word: him POS Tag: PRP
Word: down POS Tag: RP
Word: the POS Tag: DT
Word: street POS Tag: NN
Word: . POS Tag: .
```

As demonstrated, this is an easy way of achieving concurrent behavior using the Stanford pipeline.

Creating a pipeline to search text

Searching is a rich and complex topic. There are many different types of searches and approaches to perform a search. The intent here is to demonstrate how various NLP techniques can be applied to support this effort.

A single text document can be processed at one time in a reasonable time period on most machines. However, when multiple large documents need to be searched, then creating an index is a common approach to support searches. This results in a search process that completes in a reasonable period of time.

We will demonstrate one approach to create an index and then search using the index. Although the text we will use is not that large, it is sufficient to demonstrate the process.

We need to:

1. Read the text from the file
2. Tokenize and find sentence boundaries
3. Remove stop words
4. Accumulate the index statistics
5. Write out the index file

There are several factors that influence the contents of an index file:

- Removal of stop words
- Case-sensitive searches
- Finding synonyms
- Using stemming and lemmatization
- Allowing searches across sentence boundaries

We will use OpenNLP to demonstrate the process. The intent of this example is to demonstrate how to combine NLP techniques in a pipeline process to solve a search type problem. This is not a comprehensive solution and we will ignore some techniques such as stemming. In addition, the actual creation of an index file will not be presented but rather left as an exercise for the reader. Here, we will focus on how NLP techniques can be used.

Specifically, we will:

- Split the book into sentences
- Convert the sentences to lowercase
- Remove stop words
- Create an internal index data structure

We will develop two classes to support the index data structure: Word and Positions. We will also augment the StopWords class, developed in *Chapter 2, Finding Parts of Text*, to support an overloaded version of the removeStopWords method. The new version will provide a more convenient method for removing stop words.

We start with a try-with-resources block to open streams for the sentence model, en-sent.bin, and a file containing the contents of *Twenty Thousand Leagues Under the Sea* by Jules Verne. The book was downloaded from http://www.gutenberg.org/ebooks/164 and modified slightly to remove leading and trailing Gutenberg text to make it more readable:

```
try (InputStream is = new FileInputStream(new File(
        "C:/Current Books/NLP and Java/Models/en-sent.bin"));
        FileReader fr = new FileReader("Twenty Thousands.txt");
        BufferedReader br = new BufferedReader(fr)) {
        ...
} catch (IOException ex) {
    // Handle exceptions
}
```

The sentence model is used to create an instance of the SentenceDetectorME class as shown here:

```
SentenceModel model = new SentenceModel(is);
SentenceDetectorME detector = new SentenceDetectorME(model);
```

Next, we will create a string using a StringBuilder instance to support the detection of sentence boundaries. The book's file is read and added to the StringBuilder instance. The sentDetect method is then applied to create an array of sentences, as shown here:

```
String line;
StringBuilder sb = new StringBuilder();
while ((line = br.readLine()) != null) {
    sb.append(line + " ");
}
String sentences[] = detector.sentDetect(sb.toString());
```

For the modified version of the book file, this method created an array with 14,859 sentences.

Next, we used the `toLowerCase` method to convert the text to lowercase. This was done to ensure that when stop words are removed, the method will catch all of them.

```
for (int i = 0; i < sentences.length; i++) {
    sentences[i] = sentences[i].toLowerCase();
}
```

Converting to lowercase and removing stop words restricts searches. However, this is considered to be a feature of this implementation and can be adjusted for other implementations.

Next, the stop words are removed. As mentioned earlier, an overloaded version of the `removeStopWords` method has been added to make it easier to use with this example. The new method is shown here:

```
public String removeStopWords(String words) {
    String arr[] =
        WhitespaceTokenizer.INSTANCE.tokenize(words);
    StringBuilder sb = new StringBuilder();
    for (int i = 0; i < arr.length; i++) {
        if (stopWords.contains(arr[i])) {
            // Do nothing
        } else {
            sb.append(arr[i]+" ");
        }
    }
    return sb.toString();
}
```

We created a `StopWords` instance using the `stop-words_english_2_en.txt` file as shown in the following code sequence. This is one of several lists that can be downloaded from `https://code.google.com/p/stop-words/`. We chose this file simply because it contains stop words that we felt were appropriate for the book.

```
StopWords stopWords = new StopWords("stop-words_english_2_en.txt");
for (int i = 0; i < sentences.length; i++) {
    sentences[i] = stopWords.removeStopWords(sentences[i]);
}
```

The text has now been processed. The next step will be to create an index-like data structure based on the processed text. This structure will use the `Word` and `Positions` class. The `Word` class consists of fields for the word and an `ArrayList` of `Positions` objects. Since a word may appear more than once in a document, the list is used to maintain its position within the document. This class is defined as shown here:

```java
public class Word {
    private String word;
    private final ArrayList<Positions> positions;

    public Word() {
        this.positions = new ArrayList();
    }

    public void addWord(String word, int sentence,
            int position) {
        this.word = word;
        Positions counts = new Positions(sentence, position);
        positions.add(counts);
    }

    public ArrayList<Positions> getPositions() {
        return positions;
    }

    public String getWord() {
        return word;
    }
}
```

The `Positions` class contains a field for the sentence number, `sentence`, and for the position of the word within the sentence, `position`. The class definition is as follows:

```java
class Positions {
    int sentence;
    int position;

    Positions(int sentence, int position) {
        this.sentence = sentence;
        this.position = position;
    }
}
```

To use these classes, we create a `HashMap` instance to hold position information about each word in the file:

```java
HashMap<String, Word> wordMap = new HashMap();
```

The creation of the `Word` entries in the map is shown next. Each sentence is tokenized and then each token is checked to see if it exists in the map. The word is used as the key to the hash map.

The `containsKey` method determines whether the word has already been added. If it has, then the `Word` instance is removed. If the word has not been added before, a new `Word` instance is created. Regardless, the new position information is added to the `Word` instance and then it is added to the map:

```
for (int sentenceIndex = 0;
        sentenceIndex < sentences.length; sentenceIndex++) {
    String words[] = WhitespaceTokenizer.INSTANCE.tokenize(
        sentences[sentenceIndex]);
    Word word;
    for (int wordIndex = 0;
            wordIndex < words.length; wordIndex++) {
        String newWord = words[wordIndex];
        if (wordMap.containsKey(newWord)) {
            word = wordMap.remove(newWord);
        } else {
            word = new Word();
        }
        word.addWord(newWord, sentenceIndex, wordIndex);
        wordMap.put(newWord, word);
    }
}
```

To demonstrate the actual lookup process, we use the `get` method to return an instance of the `Word` object for the word "reef". The list of the positions is returned with the `getPositions` method and then each position is displayed, as shown here:

```
Word word = wordMap.get("reef");
ArrayList<Positions> positions = word.getPositions();
for (Positions position : positions) {
    System.out.println(word.getWord() + " is found at line "
        + position.sentence + ", word "
        + position.position);
}
```

The output is as follows:

```
reef is found at line 0, word 10
reef is found at line 29, word 6
reef is found at line 1885, word 8
reef is found at line 2062, word 12
```

This implementation is relatively simple but does demonstrate how to combine various NLP techniques to create and use an index data structure that can be saved as an index file. Other enhancements are possible including:

- Other filter operations
- Store document information in the `Positions` class
- Store chapter information in the `Positions` class
- Provide search options such as:
  - ° Case-sensitive searches
  - ° Exact text searches
- Better exception handling

These are left as exercises for the reader.

Summary

In this chapter, we addressed the process of preparing data and discussed pipelines. We illustrated several techniques for extracting text from HTML, Word, and PDF documents.

We showed that a pipeline is nothing more than a sequence of tasks integrated to solve some problem. We can insert and remove various elements of the pipeline as needed. The Stanford pipeline architecture was discussed in detail. We examined the various annotators that can be used. The details of this pipeline were explored along with how it can be used with multiple processors.

We demonstrated how to construct a pipeline that creates and uses an index for text searches using OpenNLP. This provided an alternate way of creating a pipeline and allowed more variation in how a pipeline can be constructed in contrast to the Stanford pipeline.

We hope this has been a fruitful introduction to NLP processing using Java. We covered all of the significant NLP tasks and demonstrated several different approaches to support these tasks using various NLP APIs. NLP is a large and complex field. We wish you the best of luck in your application development.

Index

Thank you for buying
Natural Language Processing with Java

About Packt Publishing

Packt, pronounced 'packed', published its first book, *Mastering phpMyAdmin for Effective MySQL Management*, in April 2004, and subsequently continued to specialize in publishing highly focused books on specific technologies and solutions.

Our books and publications share the experiences of your fellow IT professionals in adapting and customizing today's systems, applications, and frameworks. Our solution-based books give you the knowledge and power to customize the software and technologies you're using to get the job done. Packt books are more specific and less general than the IT books you have seen in the past. Our unique business model allows us to bring you more focused information, giving you more of what you need to know, and less of what you don't.

Packt is a modern yet unique publishing company that focuses on producing quality, cutting-edge books for communities of developers, administrators, and newbies alike. For more information, please visit our website at www.packtpub.com.

About Packt Open Source

In 2010, Packt launched two new brands, Packt Open Source and Packt Enterprise, in order to continue its focus on specialization. This book is part of the Packt Open Source brand, home to books published on software built around open source licenses, and offering information to anybody from advanced developers to budding web designers. The Open Source brand also runs Packt's Open Source Royalty Scheme, by which Packt gives a royalty to each open source project about whose software a book is sold.

Writing for Packt

We welcome all inquiries from people who are interested in authoring. Book proposals should be sent to author@packtpub.com. If your book idea is still at an early stage and you would like to discuss it first before writing a formal book proposal, then please contact us; one of our commissioning editors will get in touch with you.

We're not just looking for published authors; if you have strong technical skills but no writing experience, our experienced editors can help you develop a writing career, or simply get some additional reward for your expertise.

Natural Language Processing with Java and LingPipe Cookbook

ISBN: 978-1-78328-467-2   Paperback: 312 pages

Over 60 effective recipes to develop your Natural Language Processing (NLP) skills quickly and effectively

1. Build effective natural language processing applications.

2. Transit from ad-hoc methods to advanced machine learning techniques.

3. Use advanced techniques such as logistic regression, conditional random fields, and latent Dirichlet allocation.

Java EE Development with NetBeans 7 [Video]

ISBN: 978-1-78216-246-9   Duration: 3:08 hrs

Develop professional enterprise Java EE applications by taking advantage of the time-saving features of the NetBeans 7 IDE

1. Use the features of the popular NetBeans IDE along with keyboard shortcuts to accelerate development of Java EE applications.

2. Take advantage of the NetBeans debugger to get rid of bugs that may creep into your Java EE code.

Please check **www.PacktPub.com** for information on our titles

Java EE 7 with GlassFish 4
Application Server

Java EE 7 with GlassFish 4 Application Server

ISBN: 978-1-78217-688-6   Paperback: 348 pages

A practical guide to install and configure the GlassFish 4 application server and develop Java EE 7 applications to be deployed to this server

1. Install and configure GlassFish 4.

2. Covers all major Java EE 7 APIs and includes new additions such as JSON Processing.

3. Packed with clear, step-by-step instructions, practical examples, and straightforward explanations.

Java EE 7 Developer Handbook

Java EE 7 Developer Handbook
ISBN: 978-1-84968-794-2   Paperback: 634 pages

Develop professional applications in Java EE 7 with this essential reference guide

1. Learn about local and remote service endpoints, containers, architecture, synchronous and asynchronous invocations, and remote communications in a concise reference.

2. Understand the architecture of the Java EE platform and then apply the new Java EE 7 enhancements to benefit your own business-critical applications.

3. Learn about integration test development on Java EE with Arquillian Framework and the Gradle build system.

Please check **www.PacktPub.com** for information on our titles

Made in the USA
Middletown, DE
02 August 2015